Landscapes in Kansas

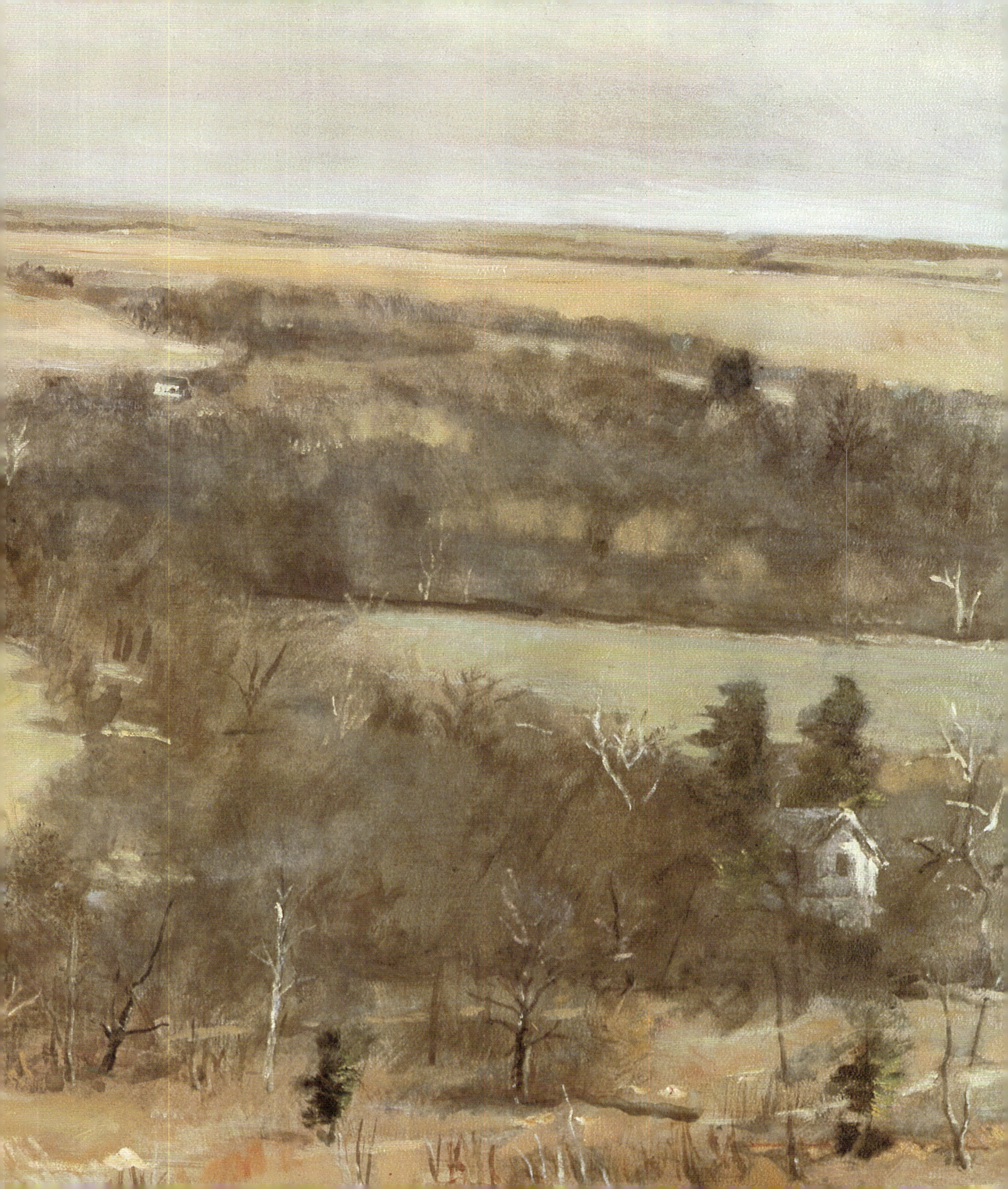

Landscapes in Kansas

Paintings by Robert Sudlow

Introduction by Lynn Bretz

University Press of Kansas

Published by the University Press of Kansas (Lawrence, Kansas 66045), which was organized by the Kansas Board of Regents and is operated and funded by Emporia State University, Fort Hays State University, Kansas State University, Pittsburg State University, the University of Kansas, and Wichita State University

FRONTISPIECE: Detail from *Windy Spring Sky*

Library of Congress Catalog Card Number: 87-40235

ISBN 0-7006-0300-X
ISBN 0-7006-0346-8 (limited edition)

Printed in Singapore by Eurasia Press (Offset) Pte. Ltd.
through Creative Graphics International, Inc. (New York)

Preface

I NEED TO MEDITATE upon the landscape. This book records some of my efforts since 1975 to stop, to find equilibrium, and to see. Closely observing my environment in Kansas has been a lifelong habit; I seem to have looked and wondered since childhood. In the process a lot of choices have been made—some instinctive, some arbitrary—and the results are embodied in what I paint and how I paint. In Kansas the seasons, weather, trees, hills, and plains always surround me. This almost commonplace landscape stirs me deeply. Frequent summers in California and sabbatical painting trips to France, Greece, England, and Ireland have offered contrast, but eastern Kansas has moved me the most and the longest.

Painting for me is a sort of communion. I have never felt comfortable with the notion that the purpose of painting is to present the way the world "looks." I paint in the midst of the landscape (often half frozen and beaten by the wind) knowing that eyes are not enough. I wish for total immersion: touch, smell, sound, and the awareness always of the swift flight of the sun. In short, to paint is to participate, to extend one's senses, to work in sympathy with an utterly mysterious cosmos. My canvases are not productions; they are imperfect recordings of a series of "happenings." Certainly much work has to be done in my studio; passages have to be simplified, enriched, or discarded. Colors must become analogies, and whole paintings have to be reconsidered. Yet most of all I struggle to bear witness to a series of particular experiences—to me this is reality. There is a line from the Spanish poet Jorge Guillén: "The landscape imagines me."

The paintings in this book, all of which are oils, are organized by seasons because I'm attracted to the notion of time as cyclic: endless change yet with recurrences. I purposely chose paintings dating from the last decade to echo this pattern. A large majority of the work included here deals with autumn and winter. Sparseness appeals to me. The range of locale is not extensive. Those who search my paintings for identifiable landmarks may look in vain. Various fields, ditches, ponds, hedgerows, hills, and farms may seem familiar, but they have undergone much metamorphosis prior to their appearance on my canvases. I suspect that they are more typical than specific as a result. To accompany the paintings, I have selected a few entries from my journals. Although not necessarily contemporary with the painting, the entries reflect upon my ongoing communion with the Kansas landscape.

I want to acknowledge Anna Bloch's faithful encouragement and the help of Douglas Keller and of Georgia and Jack Olsen of the American Legacy Gallery, Kansas City, Missouri. This book is dedicated to my wife, Barbara, who accompanies me on these missions.

Robert Sudlow
Spring 1987

Introduction
by Lynn Bretz

ARTIST ROBERT SUDLOW PROTESTS, in all seriousness, that he paints not the four but the twenty seasons of Kansas. Experience teaches him that Kansas weather eschews the quartet of seasons that come and go with wall-calendar regularity. So do not expect this book of Kansas landscapes to be neatly quartered into spring, summer, autumn, and winter. In fact, though an art critic has tagged this best-known contemporary Kansas landscapist a "land-locked Monet," Sudlow rejects the comparison, because Claude Monet's studies of the precise light that a certain hour of the day throws on a haystack could never be carried out in Kansas. Here, one day looks as if sent from one world, the next day from another. Kansas seasons are impulsive and fluid forms, given to false starts and curious transitions, Sudlow says. For a painter, that means the subject is never the same—a fact of his landscapist life that Sudlow treasures.

Sudlow speaks frequently of "Kansas' changefulness," and it is one of the astute notions about the Kansas landscape found in the fifty-four paintings reproduced in this book. To Sudlow's regionwide following, his large canvases conjure the temperamental skies and woolly fields that imbue Kansas with a free-spirited vitality. His viewers say that their eyes are opened to a world they had ignored. As *Kansas City Star* art critic Donald Hoffmann has noted, Sudlow has "elevated the very way we see the landscape, too often dismissed as dull."

With a hunter's eye for secluded spaces, Sudlow for the past sixteen years has scouted and staked out sites in the raw and untrimmed countryside of Douglas, Chase, and Wabaunsee counties, three counties in the eastern third of the state. He has painted in the bitter winds of winter and the stalwart gusts of spring, roping his canvas to a bush or nailing it to a tree. On occasion, he has suffered the panic of the outdoorsman who, mesmerized by adventures in the wild, suddenly comes untranced, realizing the dangers of being in a brewing winter storm in remote country. The Flint Hills ranchers who have opened their gates to Sudlow identify with the physical demands of painting *en plein air*, tramping through the mud and brush and braving the weather. Like these ranchers, whom he admires, Sudlow is emotionally attached to this land that is out of the immediate reach and the minds of most Kansans.

Sudlow sees a kinship between himself and the Orientals, who considered landscapes the artist's wellspring. Like them, he senses that the land is a living entity, that rocks are its bones, streams its arteries. Chronicling on canvas this visceral Kansas spirit and its spontaneity is no passive act; it becomes a dialogue. "The world is animate and alive," Sudlow says, "and it's observing me as much as I'm observing it. Behind all my work is this sense of an invisible reality."

This dialogue speaks to Kansans and exiled Kansans, as Elizabeth Broun, chief curator of the Smithsonian Museum of American Art, has discovered. She has seen Sudlow landscapes gracing some unusual places, such as Greenwich Village apartments. The paintings travel to foreign climes, she suspects, because "the owners felt his work embodied some quality of the state or the Midwest which they never left behind no matter how far afield they went."

CHASE AND WABAUNSEE COUNTIES belong to the comely Flint Hills. On a map the Flint Hills make a peanut-shaped imprint stretching several hundred miles from northern Oklahoma to northern Kansas. Close up it is a region thick with unique visual textures. Here grows one of the last stands of tallgrass prairie. A beauty among these high prairie grasses is the bluestem, which in Sudlow's landscapes glints like a gem changing colors under different lights and seasons—golden, pink, red, ochre, charcoal, or blue green. The land is also rough, strewn with flint and limestone.

Sudlow often views the Flint Hills from a hillside looking across a valley. The hills just beyond the valley do not appear to recede; instead, they seem poised like cresting waves, pictured at the instant before they roll forward. In places whole stretches of the hills undulate like ocean waves, revealing a secret from Kansas' geologic past—that it once was an inland sea. Sudlow confesses, "The seaward roll of this landscape is my greatest joy."

In Chase and Wabaunsee counties, the sky looms. As a member of the Coronado expedition wrote in the mid-1500s at first sight from these hills, you have a sense of standing on land shaped like some huge ball, with sky encircling it. Likewise, in Sudlow's Flint Hills works, the point of view almost seems to be from some place aloft, as though he had painted from a hot-air balloon—a prop he half-seriously considers acquiring.

In sparse areas of the Flint Hills, the undulating ground and swollen skies play havoc with perspective. They provide phantasms. "Sometimes there are no trees," says Sudlow. "You see something and the effect is hallucinating. You don't know if it's a cow or a schoolhouse or a rock because the scale is mysterious."

Mirrorlike, lakes and ponds pick up incredible colors from the sky. So in another Flint Hills spatial illusion, Sudlow finds himself seeing the whole tawny landscape as though it floats around the sky and its reflections.

The Flint Hills give rise to other curious features, such as the flat-topped bluff, a formation that can be mistaken for the ancient Indian burial sites that have been found in this region. These mysterious, stark bluffs fascinate Sudlow, as do the valleys that are veined with coffee-colored streams rolling along wonderfully white gravel bars; the water attracts huddles of cottonwood, oak, walnut, hickory, and elm. The valleys strike Sudlow as quotes lifted from the Barbizon artists' pictures of the Fontainebleau forest in the mid-nineteenth century.

In the Flint Hills, Sudlow finds himself investigating over and over the theme and variation of "infinitude." But in Douglas County, east of the Flint Hills, the topography suggests a variety of themes. It is a richly varied terrain, a place where hybrids cross paths, where different species of birds congregate, where flora and fauna interdigitate, as the biologists say; it is a place where you find both tree-lined hills and patches of prairie grass, fertile valleys and knobby, rock-strewn ridges. Douglas County leads a more urban existence; you'll find no vast stretches of ranchland here. But from the vantage points that Sudlow prefers around Vinland, Baldwin, Lone Star, and other small towns, the farms or other man-made structures are often subject to the camouflages of nature, such as winter's icy drape.

Just south of Lawrence, county seat of Douglas, is a place that Sudlow and his University of Kansas landscape painting students know as "the red field"—a large sweep of bluestem prairie grass angled on a hill and enclosed by trees. Sudlow thinks of it as "a piece of the Flint Hills in captivity." It's proof of Sudlow's observation that Douglas County is a microcosm.

All of this is not to suggest that Sudlow gives us accurate descriptions of Chase, Wabaunsee, and Douglas counties' physical features in a photorealist or strict realist style. The authenticity that Sudlow's landscapes convey doesn't rely on exquisite detail. His style is that of an impressionist. Rarely can you look at one of his paintings and name specific plants, trees, birds, or rocks—though Sudlow knows their distinctions. He prefers to suggest an object, not detail it. Cows may be, as he says, "little dots that look very cowlike."

Sudlow will, according to mood, add or delete a farmhouse: "Sometimes I'll improvise right there while I'm looking at the landscape. I'll alter the whole configuration. The skies will change in a mysterious way, and I'll try to pick out what will suggest that movement." And when his wife, Barbara, hands him her photograph of the view he painted, Sudlow will struggle to identify it. Her photographs have shown him buildings and power lines that his eyes never saw. He was too intent on some deep plane in the landscape.

The artist convinces us with other visual improvisations. Sudlow's snow, never pure "white," shimmers with blues, reds, and yellows. This is one reason why he greatly prefers to paint in winter, when luminous whites refract a wondrous array of colors in the "muted" landscape. On a canvas painted in late winter in isolated Martin Park, on the outskirts of Lawrence, Sudlow's thick brushwork of snow carries a bright pink spot. An impetuous stroke, Sudlow says. It's not realistic, but the eye accepts it.

Sudlow's paintings are, for some, like Rorschach tests. In one of his Flint Hills landscapes, for example, a winter blast has come and gone, and enough warmth has returned to suggest that the scene will go into a thaw—a transformation apparent in a battle fought by cool and warm tones. The struggle yields strange shapes. The viewer is encouraged to wonder what force cast those shapes and light. Sudlow wants us to "read" the canvas in this way, to search it and let the imagination complete the picture.

His landscapes are not "about" a frozen moment in time on a Kansas hillside. A static scene does not satisfy him. Just as he is caught up in light and the colors it brings, so he is concerned with how that light and color change over time. He attempts to chronicle the visual events of several hours—usually an afternoon's span. He compares his approach to Cézanne's, which demanded that we look from several different planes or points of view all at once. With Sudlow, we look at several different times and moods of a changeful Kansas day.

IN KANSAS, landscape painting is flourishing. In part, we owe this to a revival that took place in the late sixties, when Americans were re-identifying with the land. At that time, a political/environmental groundswell, the ecology movement, had taken hold. It disputed the credo that the fast lane led downtown and dusty roads nowhere, that urban sprawl was somehow superior to undeveloped countryside. A generation of Americans romanticized about getting "back to the land." In Kansas, conservationists moved to preserve in a park a piece of our magnificent prairie. In the art world, "forgotten" landscape artists, snubbed since mid-century by museums and galleries, re-emerged. Although out of fashion, the landscapists had been painting all along. That became apparent in the art exhibit "A Sense of Place: American Artists and the Land," which toured the country in the early seventies, reminding us of the tradition of landscape painting. Organized by painter and Hudson River conservationist Allen Gussow, "A Sense of Place" featured artists from the nineteenth century to the present who saw and painted expressions of the land. As poet Richard Wilbur wrote in the catalog introduction, our nation has a legacy of artists who never succumbed to the myopia of seeing nature as little more than a "smear of green."

But the current attention in Kansas to landscape painting can also be attributed to native son Robert Sudlow. Three works by Sudlow hung in "A Sense of Place" when it opened in Nebraska at the Joslyn Art Museum and Sheldon Memorial Art Gallery in 1972. The Sudlows reproduced in this book have been painted since that exhibit. They belong to a large collection that testifies that Sudlow's past sixteen years have been fertile ones, and their sphere of influence has touched many contemporary regional landscapists.

Since 1945, Sudlow has taught at the University of Kansas. Art majors and area painters have taken his landscape painting course, during which Sudlow instructs them not only in painting but also in painting outdoors in Kansas. He shows them Flint Hills overlooks, like a favorite of his near Bazaar, where the uplands hold suggestions of Indian burial mounds and where bluestem prairie grass carpets everything. He imparts some of the lessons he learned years ago from his teachers at the University of Kansas: Raymond Eastwood, the late Karl Mattern, and the late Albert Bloch. André Lhote was his instructor during Parisian studies in the early fifties, and he worked with Richard Diebenkorn in the late fifties.

But none of these mentors or instructors has plumbed the Kansas landscape as deeply as Sudlow. It could be said that his serious study of Kansas began in the early 1970s, when he discovered how crucial it was to spend most of his painting time outdoors, seeing, breathing, and feeling the elements of the landscape. But in another sense, Sudlow has been painting, in his mind's eye, Kansas landscapes since his youth in Holton. Even today, he remembers in exact detail the contours of the lawn at his family home. And like many Kansans, he grew to love the sight of broad horizontal spaces, a preference comparable to the ocean lover's fondness for the whiff of salt air.

Though Sudlow has painted hundreds of landscapes, his subject constantly shows new faces to him. He is quick to remind followers that in his concentrated forays into only 3 of the 105 counties in Kansas, he has hardly begun to probe the range of the state's varied contours. And seasons? Winters, especially, continue to show him inexhaustible possibilities. The luminous skies offer great challenges, too. Sudlow believes he has never quite captured on canvas that fluid yet palpable quality of light-filled, dense, and shimmery air. And he hopes to paint the Kansas sky just as darkness arrives. The cloak that falls at dark is full of color, he contends. Like the seasons and sites of Kansas, the last rays of one day never look like any other.

Winter

A quick-dropping sun. Every pressing twilight overtakes my half-formed plans. Night follows night and there is little time to savor the winter light. The cold burnished radiance is so quickly extinguished. Can I remember?

Across the evening landscape, between the settled farmyards a measure of original wildness still persists. The calling owl gives witness.

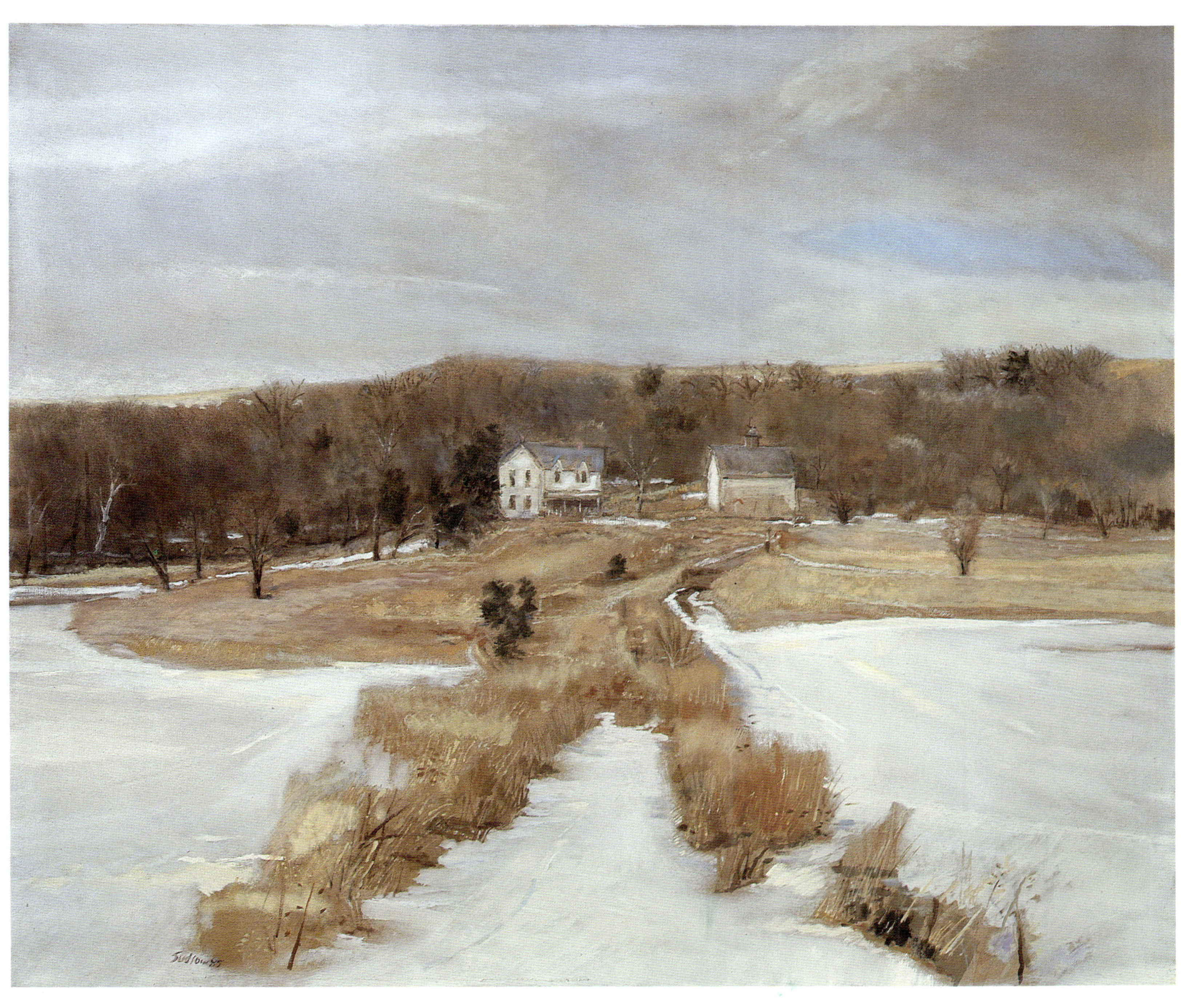

1. *Abandoned Farm, Winter, 1985,* 42″ × 50″
American Legacy Gallery, Kansas City, Missouri

2. *Bazaar Overlook #2, 1981,* 50″ × 45″
American Legacy Gallery, Kansas City, Missouri

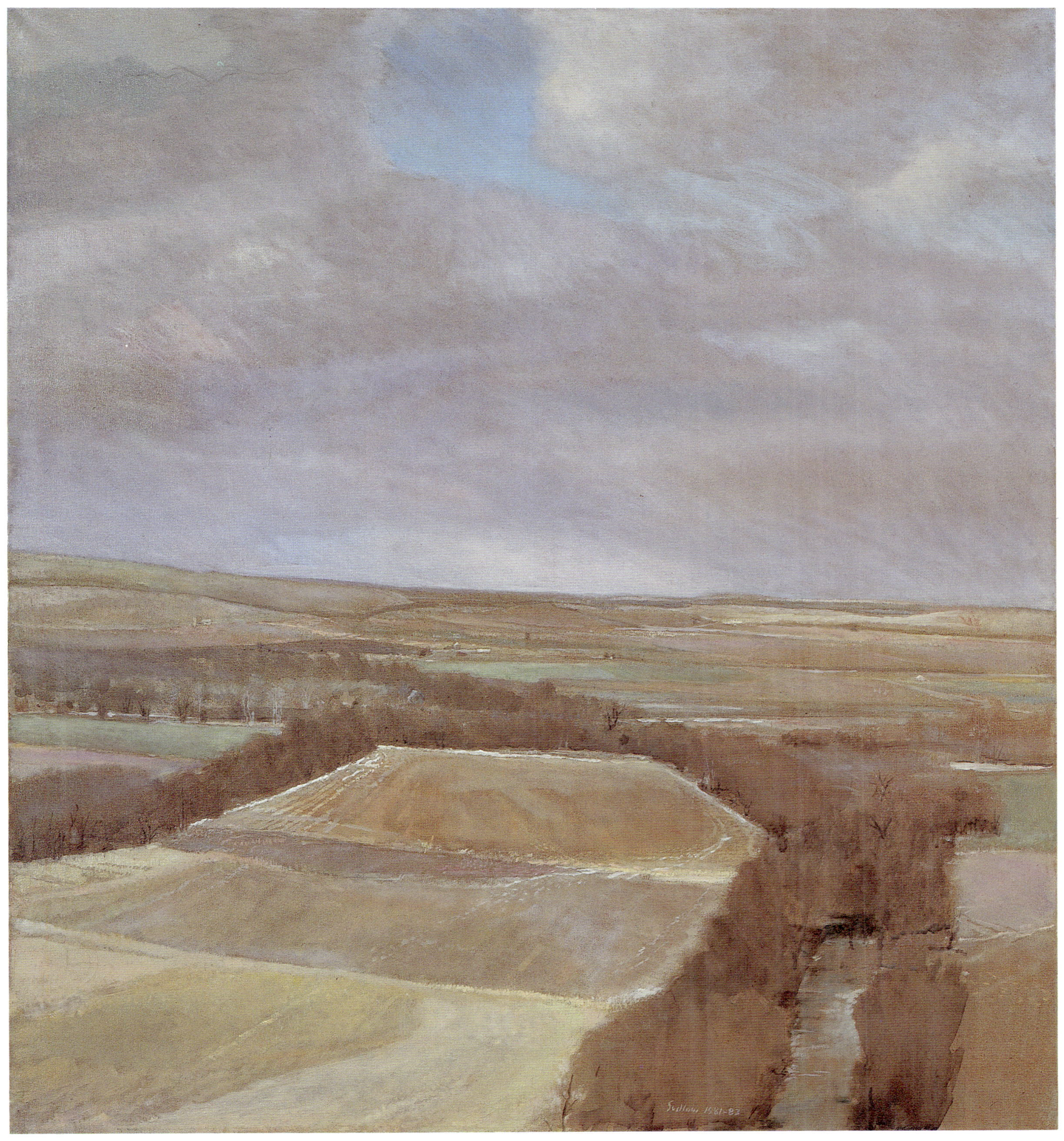

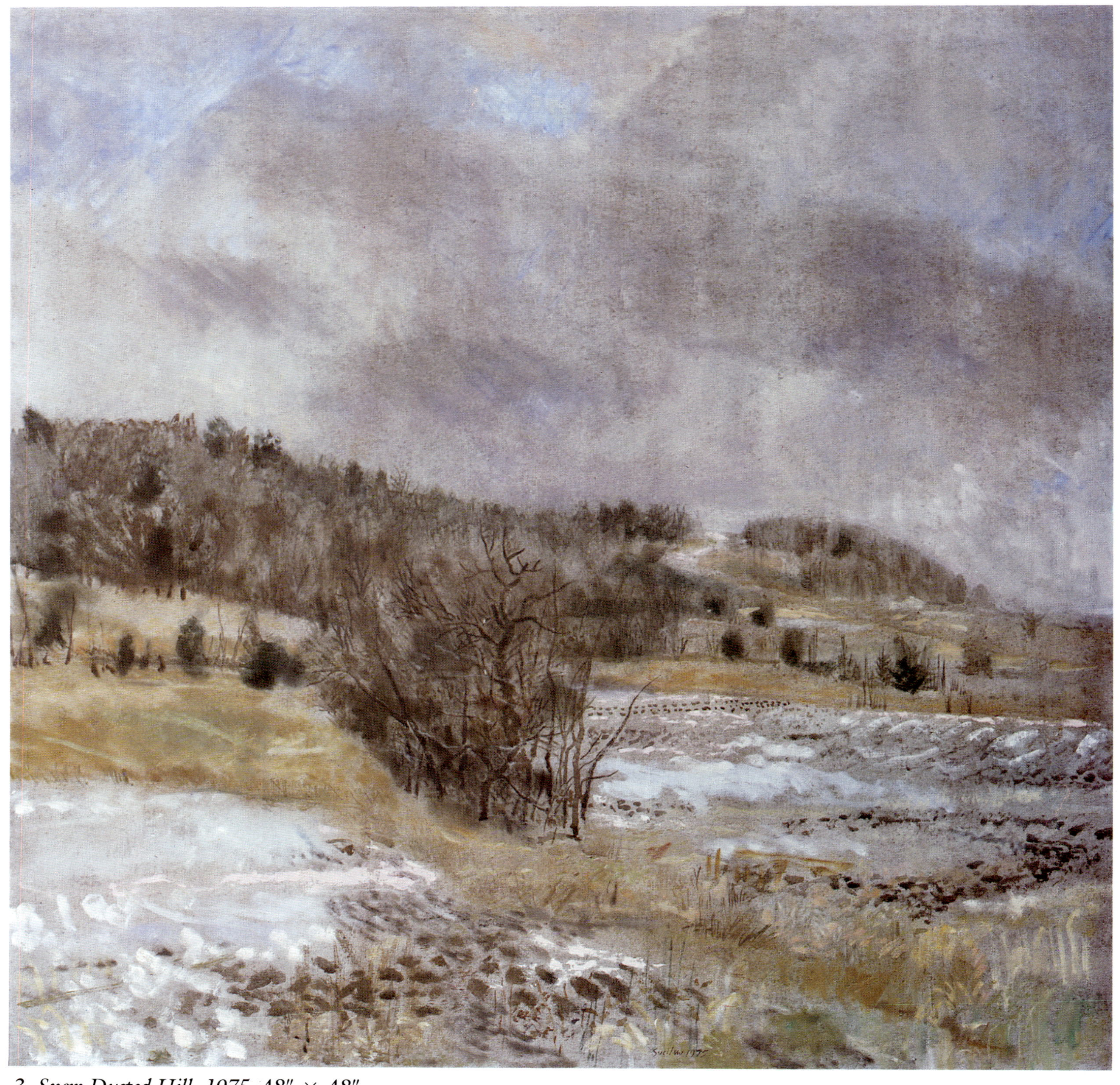

3. *Snow-Dusted Hill, 1975,* 48″ × 48″
Collection of Mr. & Mrs. Peter Whiteknight, Lawrence, Kansas

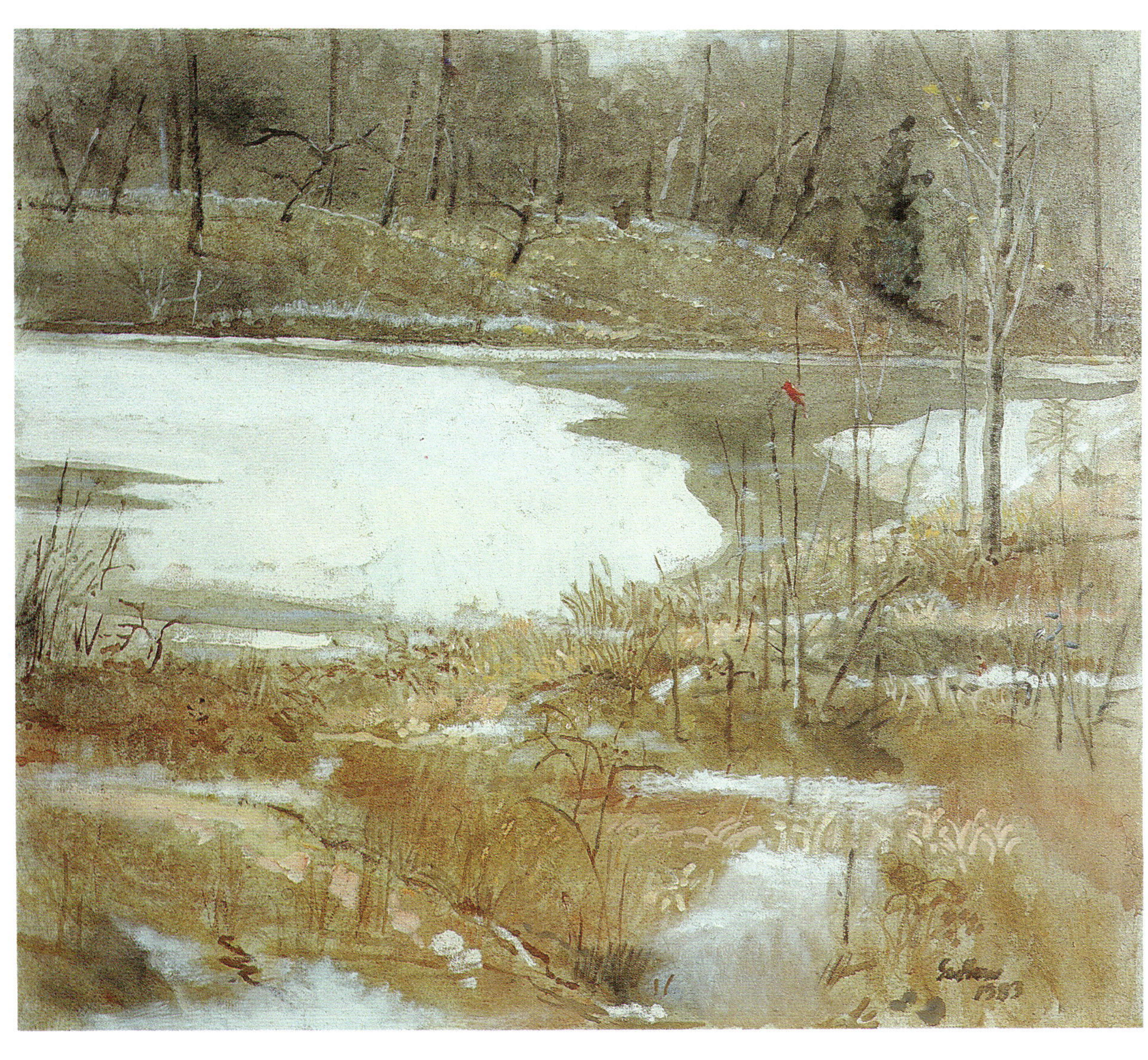

4. *Winter, Lessenden Pond, 1982,* 22″ × 22″
Private Collection

5. *Snowy Hill and Windy Sky, 1978,* 46″ × 44″
Topeka Public Library

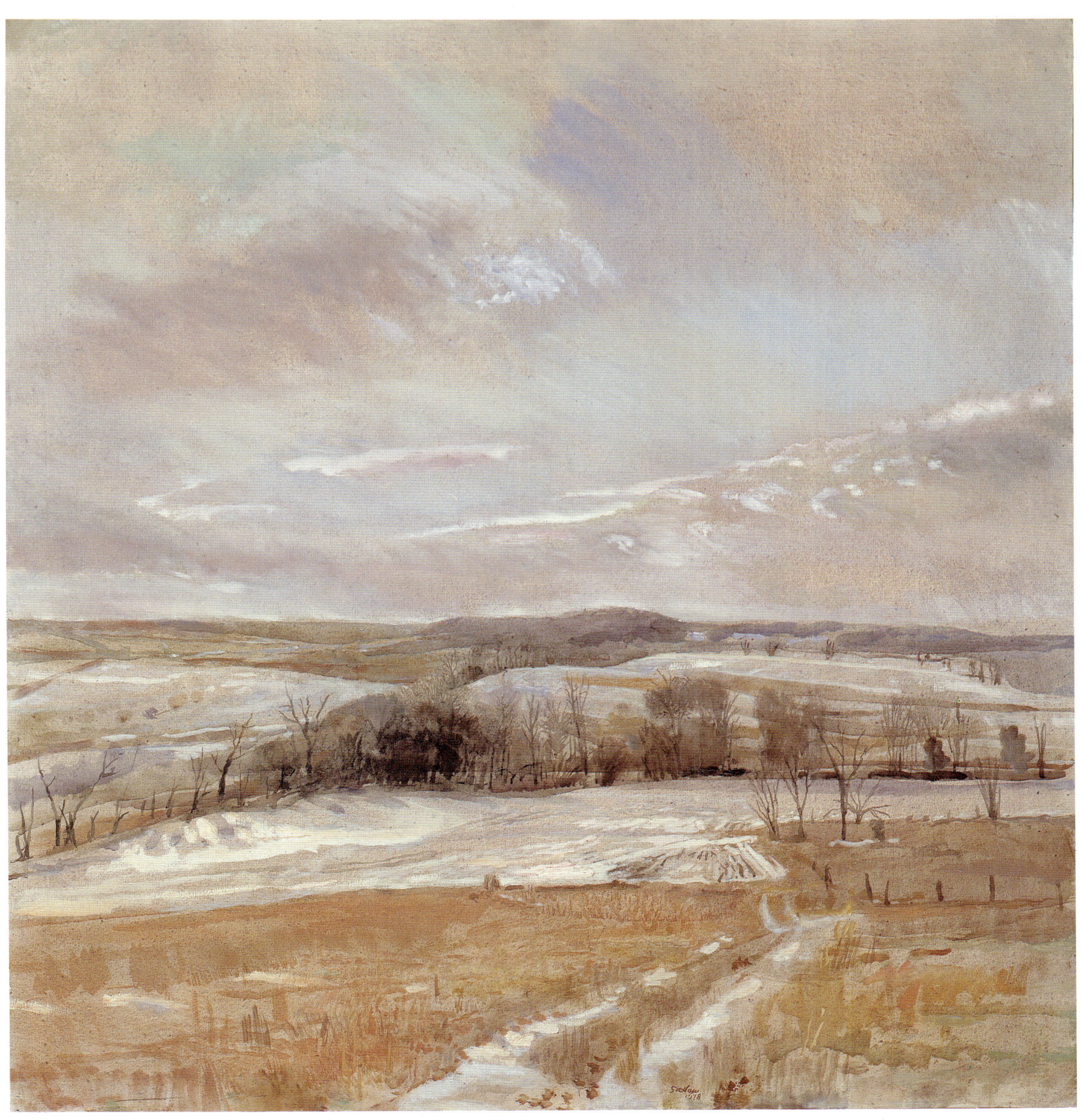

I can think of no more moving sight than sunlight through a thistlehead or pale winter grass blazing with a glory I can never paint. These ordinary things lead me, and my canvases get tangled in roadside ditches, weeds, and brambles.

Studio paintings so often wilt, grow stale, that I must constantly go out-of-doors; the nearest hedgerow can overwhelm me in a new flowerbed of paint. These paintings are a part of this renewal process. Now they seem lacking in formal solutions, but they are all eager traps for the unexpected—and they were all painted outside.

My pigments and canvas never do very well at imitating nature, that trick or technique that mimics the camera is not convincing. What holds savor for me is a host of invisibles—the wind, the smell of earth, or that incredible sense of presence that the seasons bring.

Perhaps all artistic pretexts fail in the midst of natural forces. At best it is an uncomfortable confrontation; paint turns to sludge, and the best-laid plans fall apart. I know that sometimes my head gets full of the sky; the earth is transformed. Perhaps this is why I am always painting.

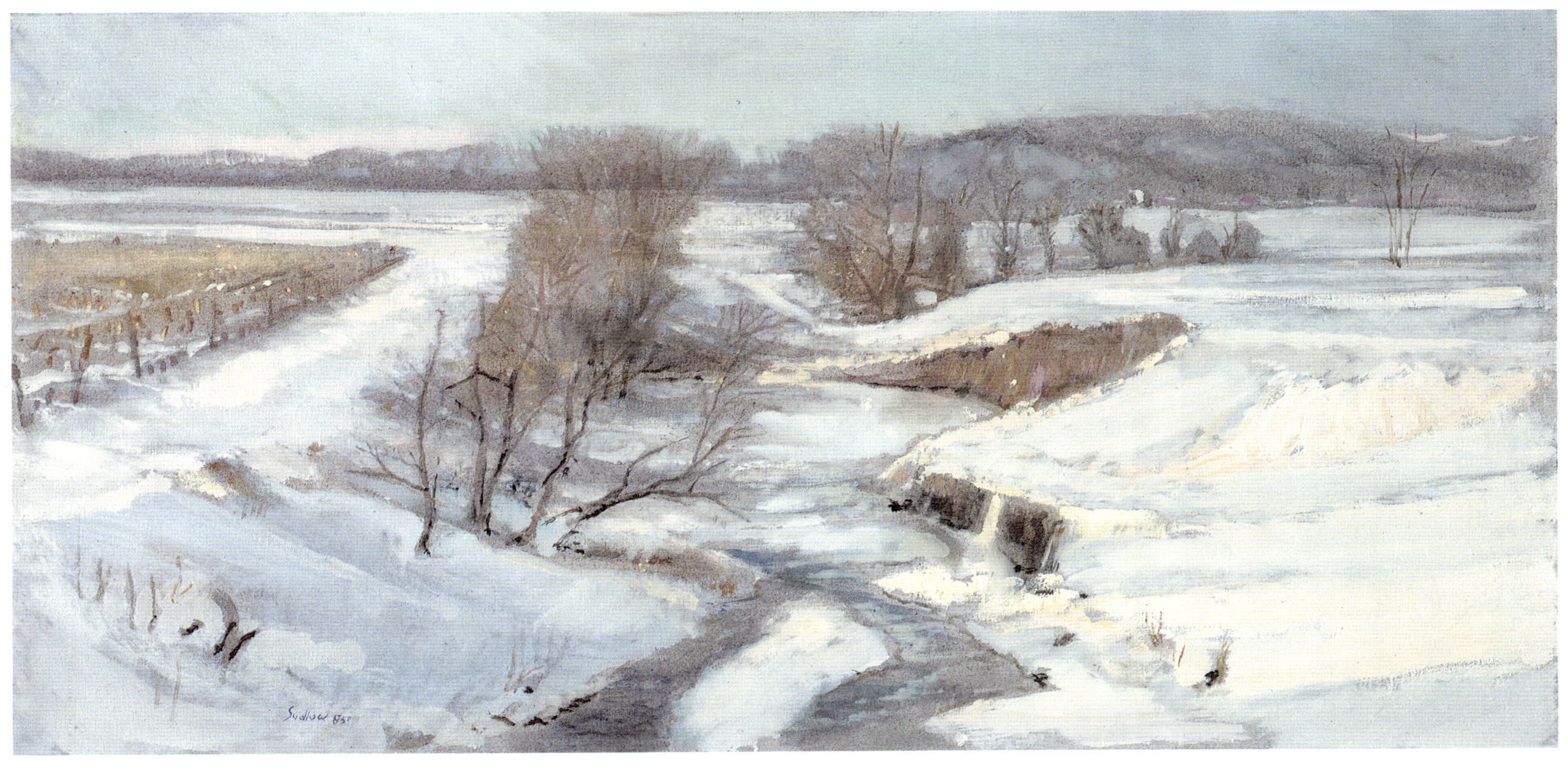

6. *Snowy Markley Stream, 1985,* 18″ × 36″
Collection of Mr. & Mrs. James Connely, Lawrence, Kansas

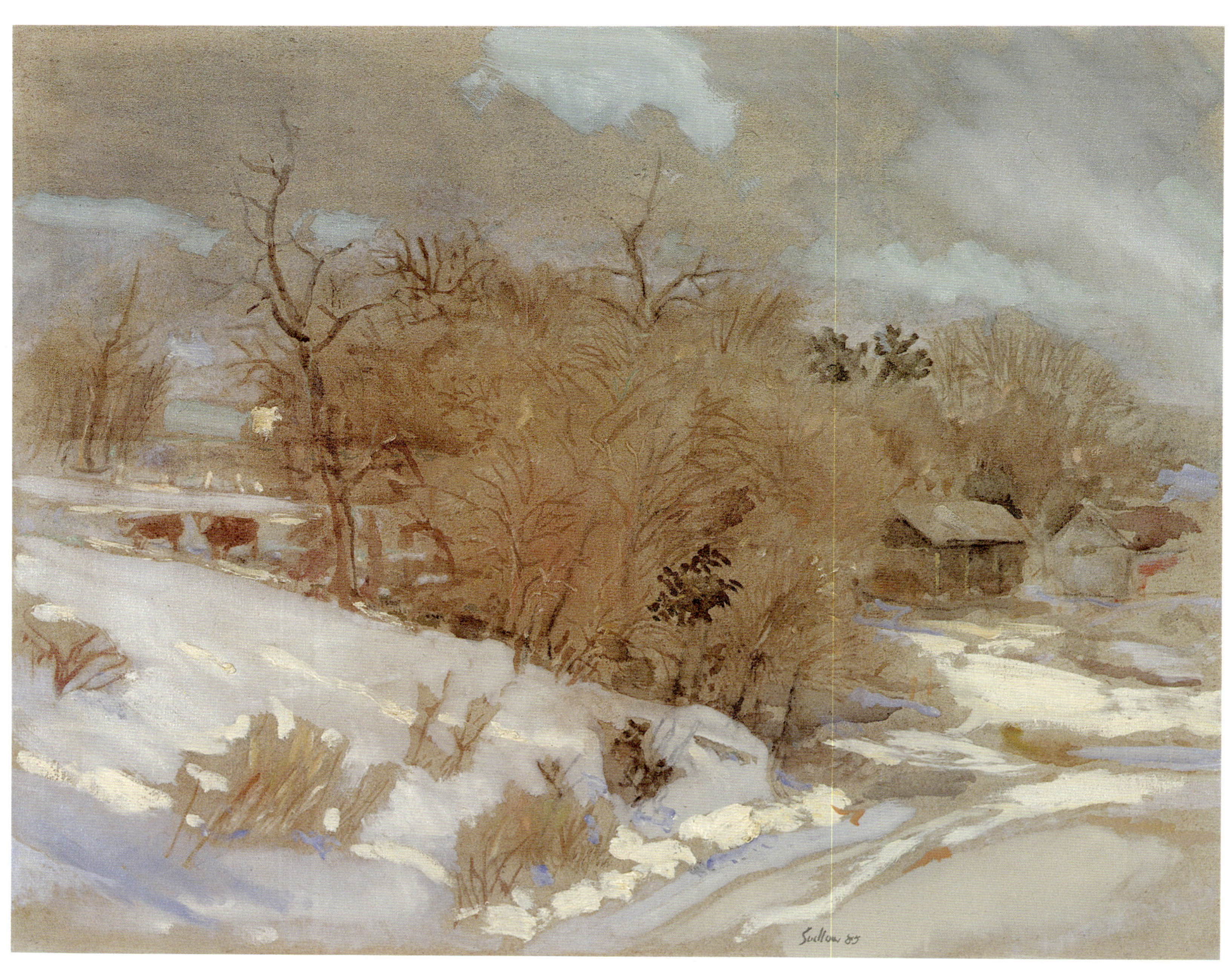

7. *Lucken's Farm, 1985,* 20″ × 25″
Collection of Mr. & Mrs. Robert C. Hamilton, Leawood, Kansas

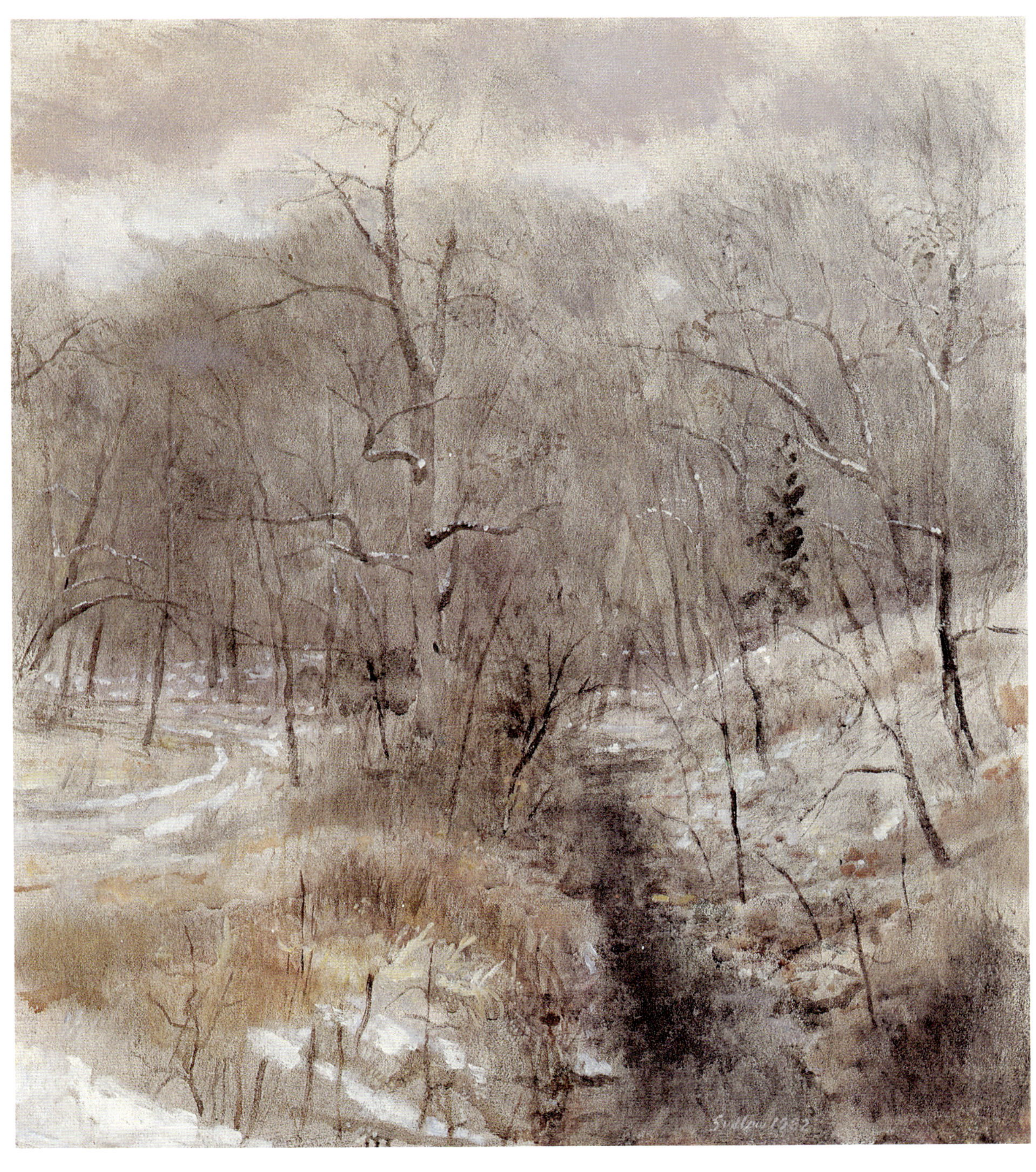

8. *Snowy Wood, 1982,* 30″ × 27½″
Collection of Mr. & Mrs. Peter Whiteknight, Lawrence, Kansas

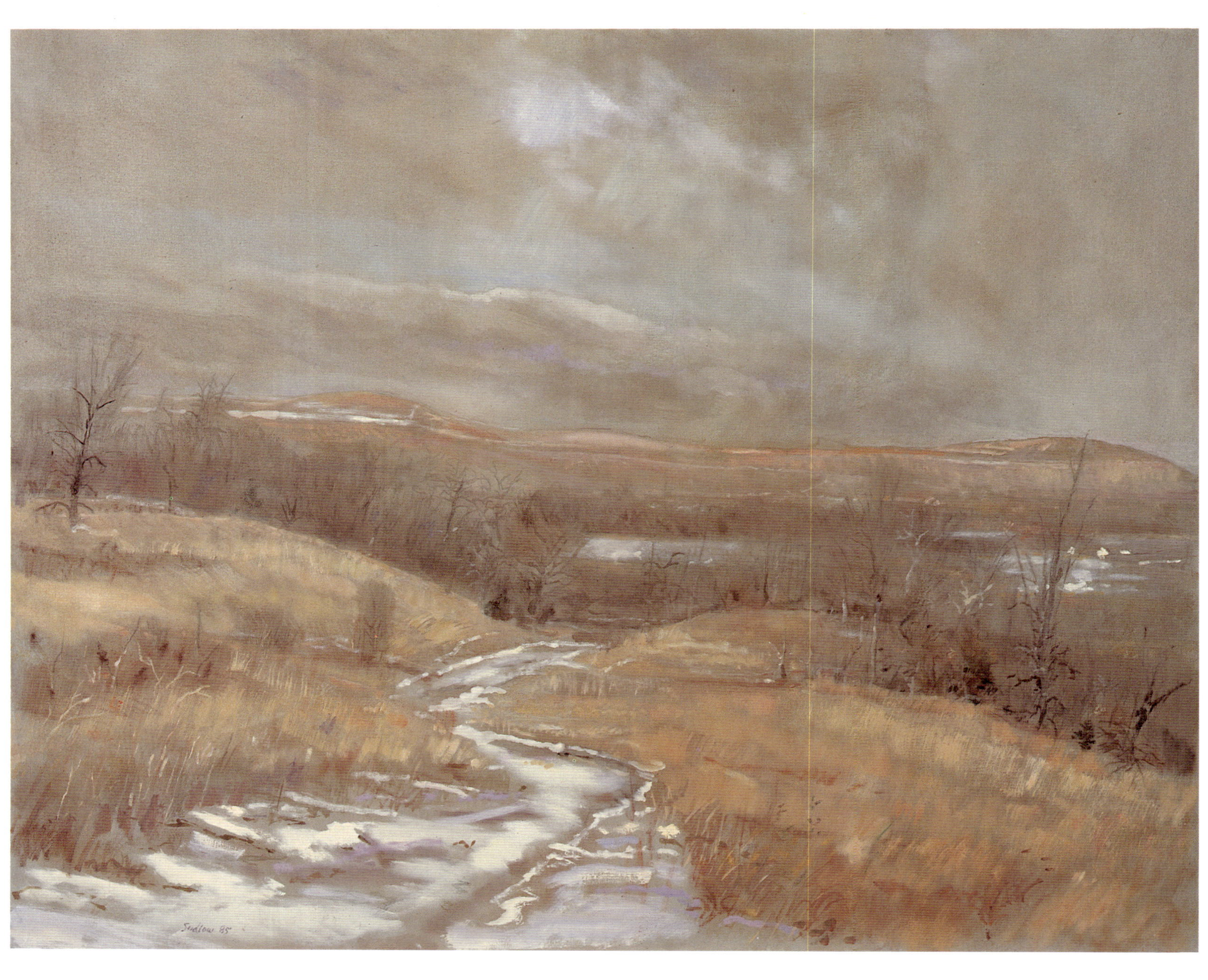

9. *Winter Storm, Hessdale, 1985,* 40″ × 50″
Collection of Dr. Virginia J. Savin, Shawnee Mission, Kansas

10. *Frozen Duck Pond, 1985,* 50″ × 45″
Kellas Gallery, Lawrence, Kansas

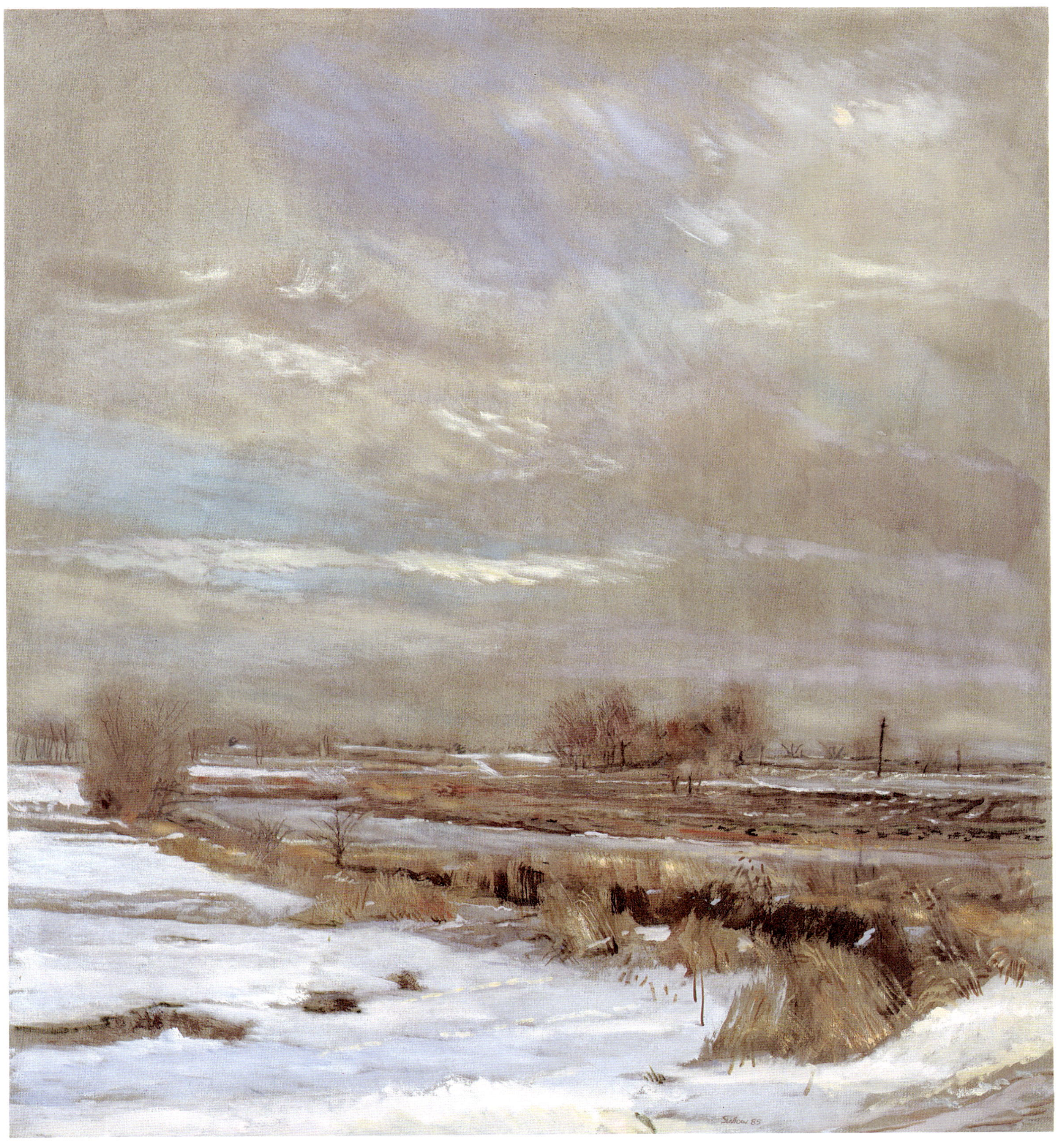

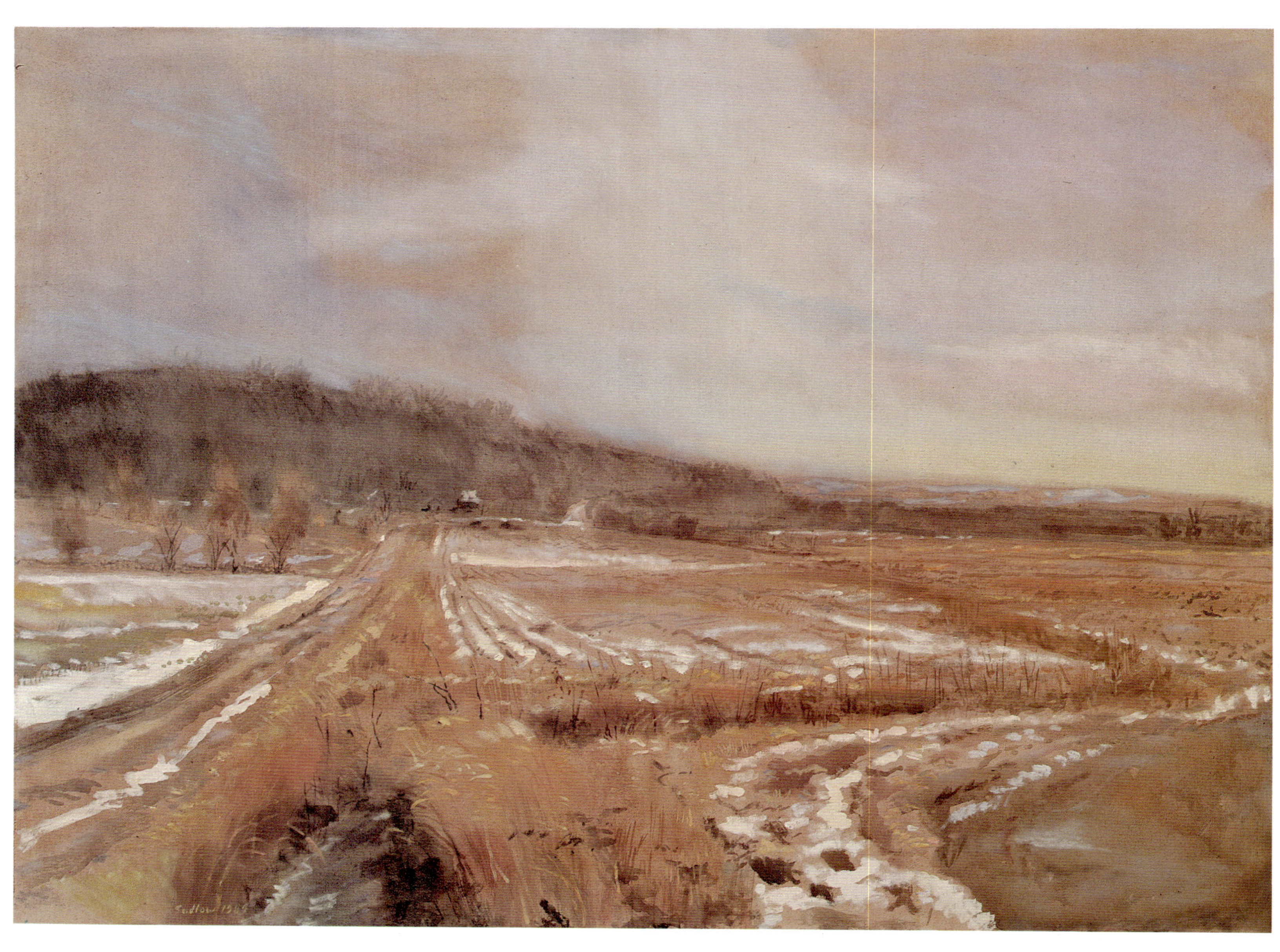

11. *Melting Snow Fields, 1985,* 40″ × 50″
Private Collection

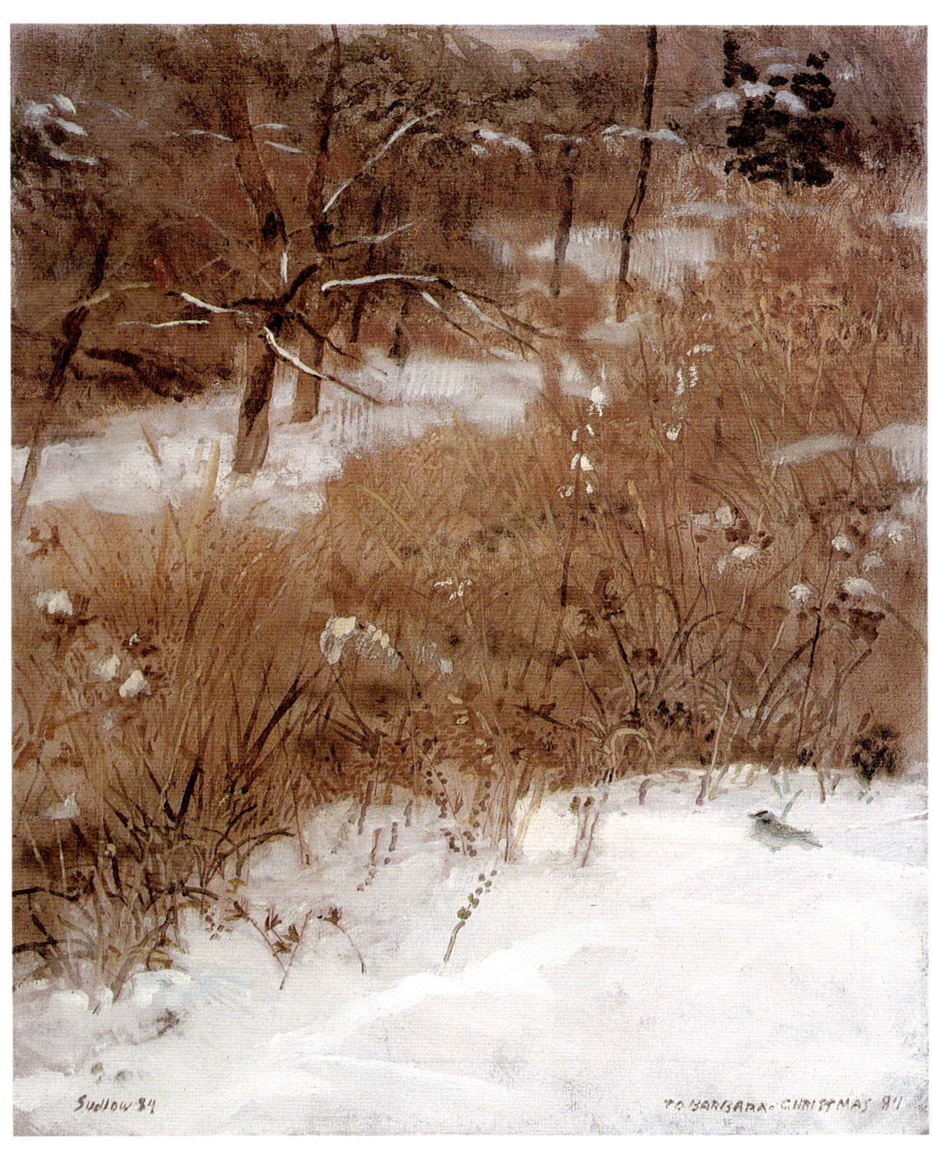

12. *Snow Bird, 1984,* 25″ × 20″
Collection of Barbara Sudlow, Lawrence, Kansas

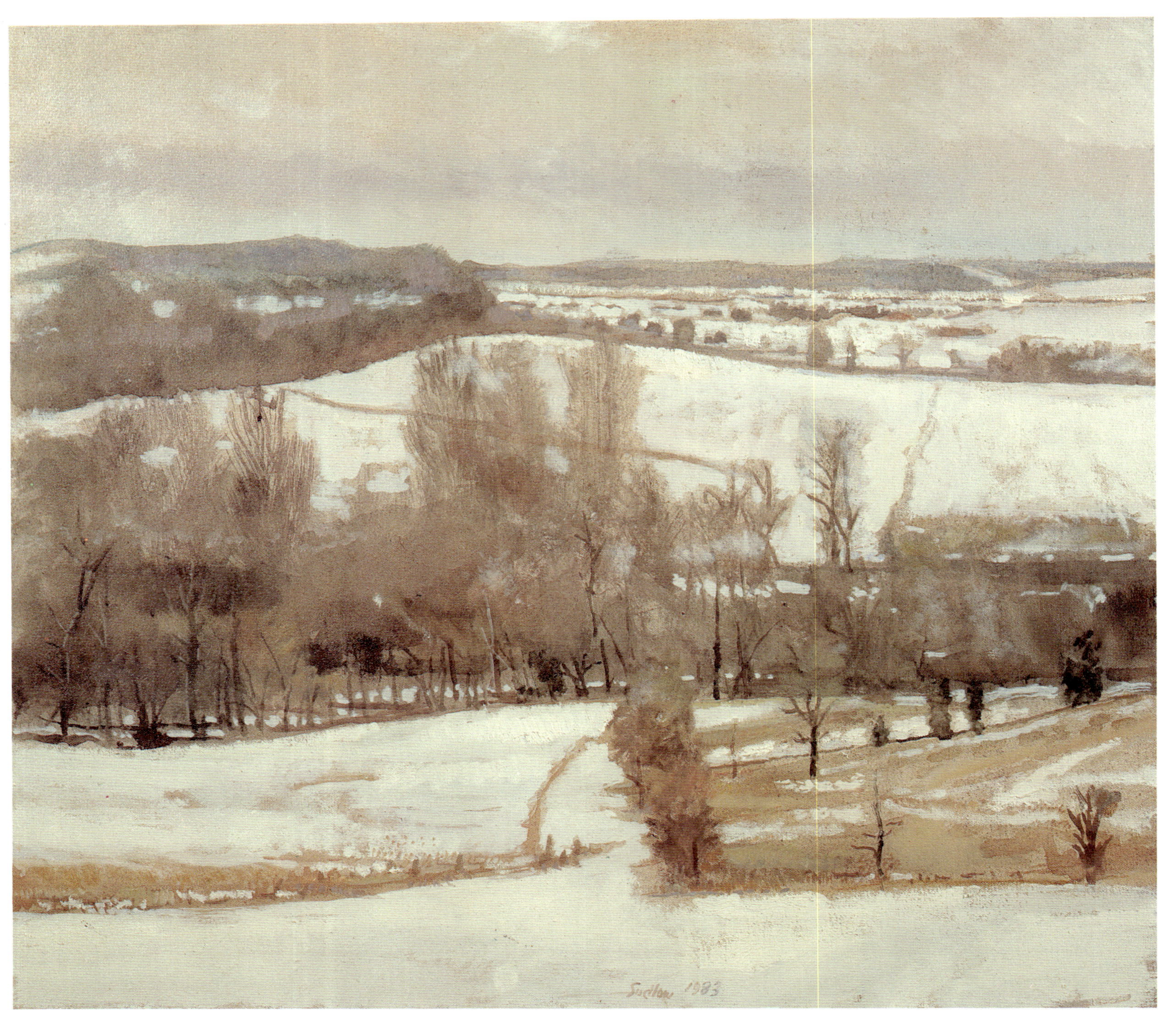

13. *Winter, Hidden Valley, 1980,* 28″ × 32″
Private Collection

14. *Winter Road, 1981,* 54″ × 48″
Artist's Collection

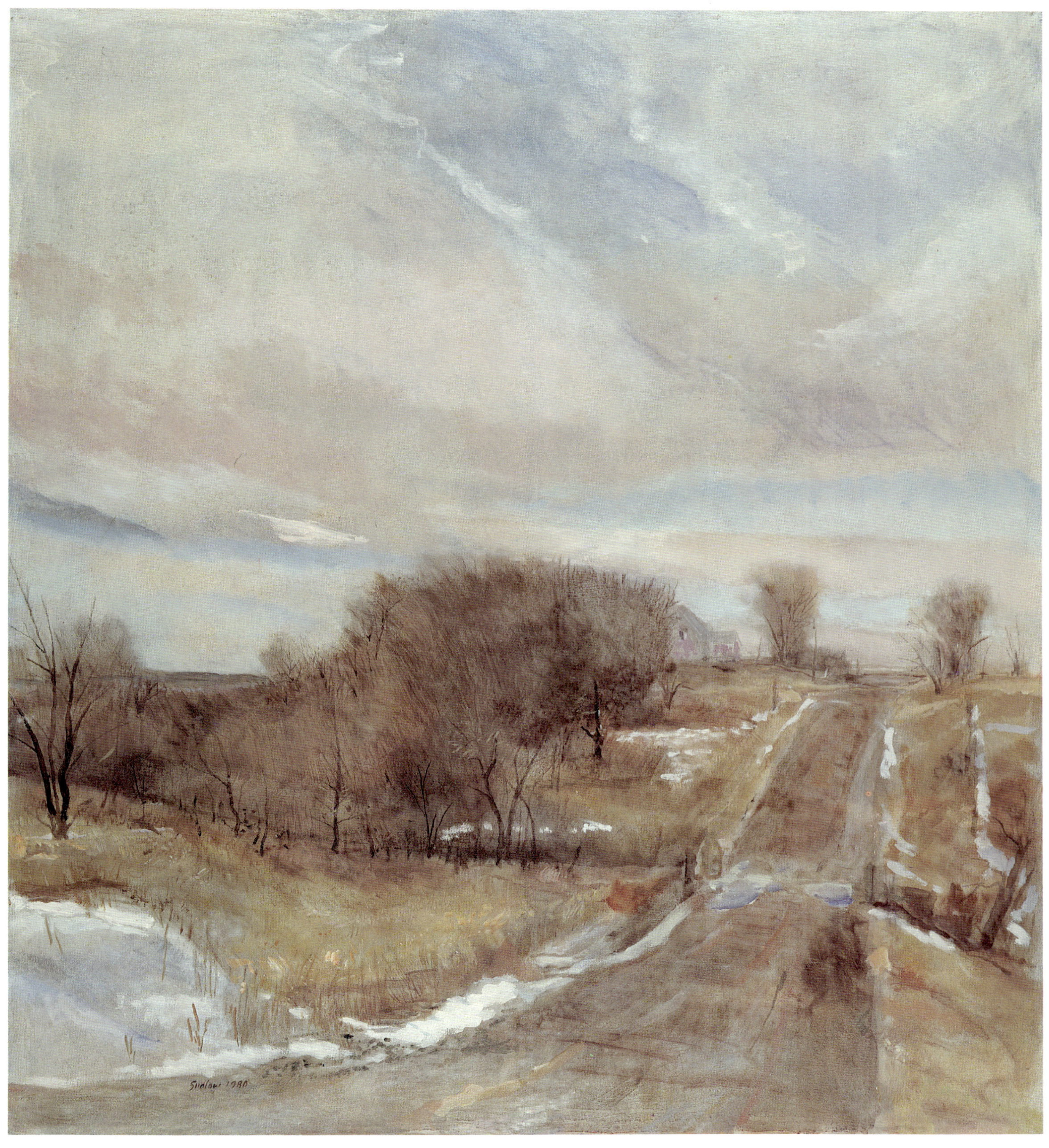
Sudlow 1980

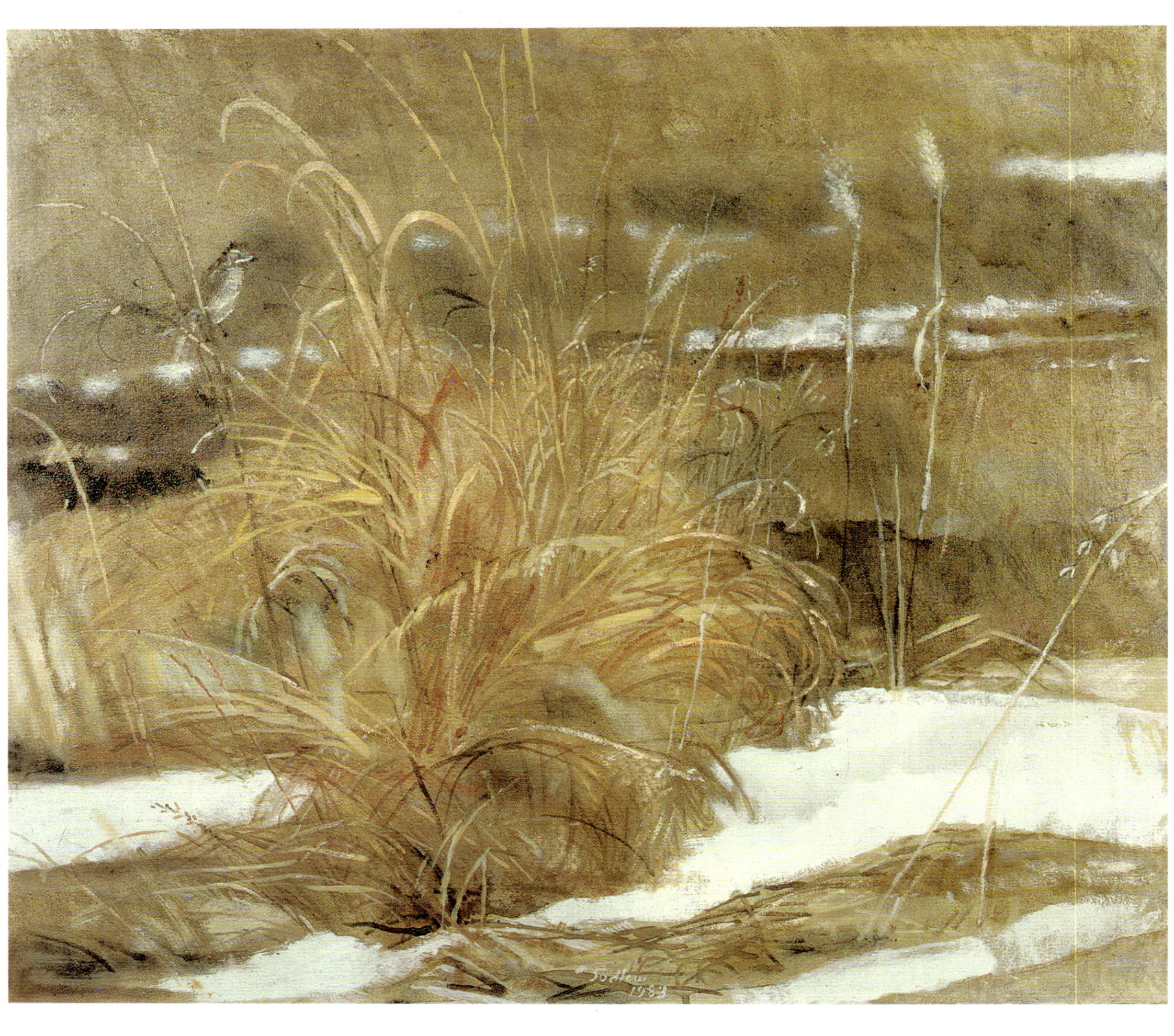

15. *Winter Grass and Sparrow, 1983,* 26″ × 30″
Private Collection

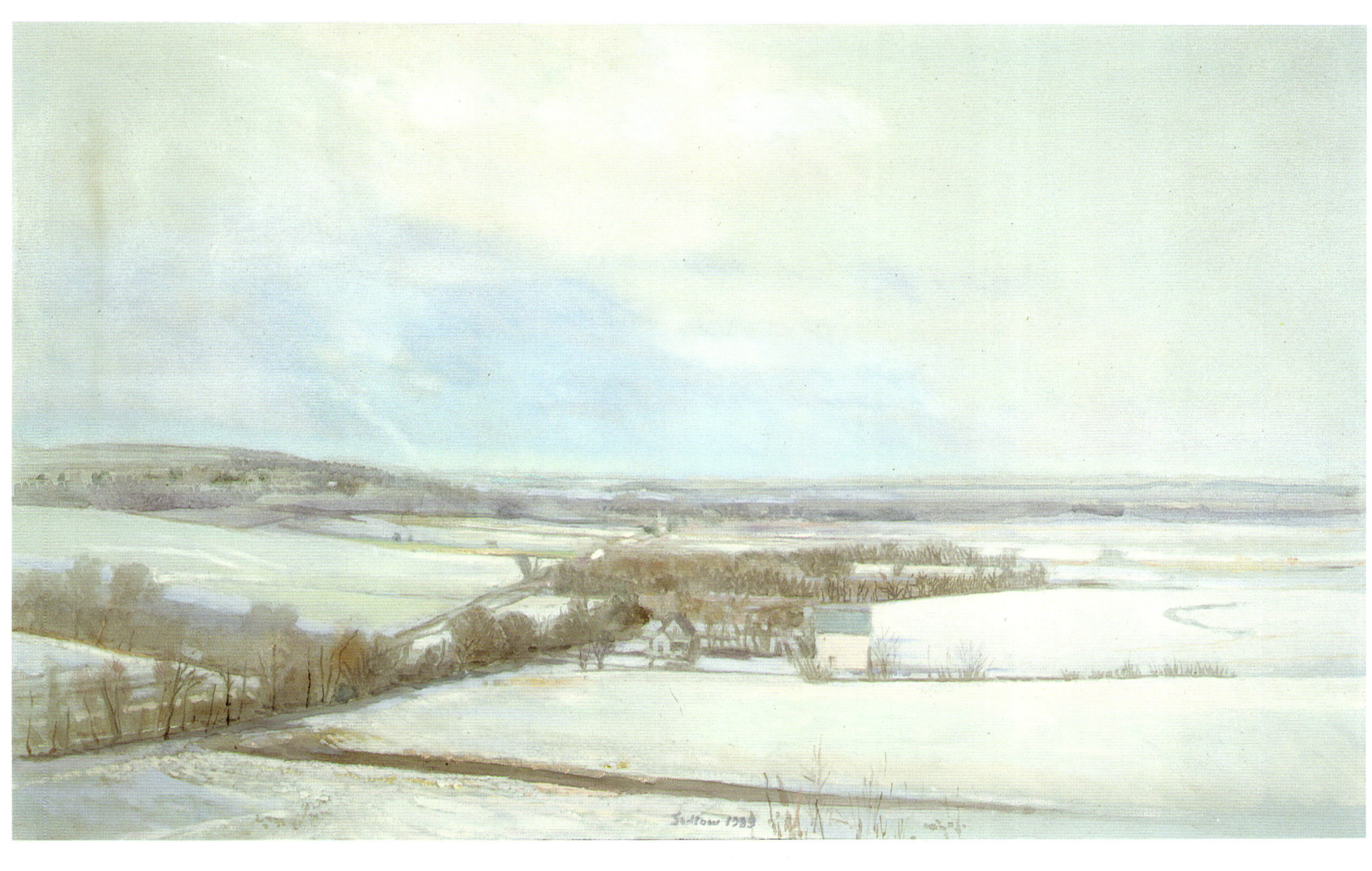

16. *Northview Winter, 1983,* 28″ × 45″
Private Collection

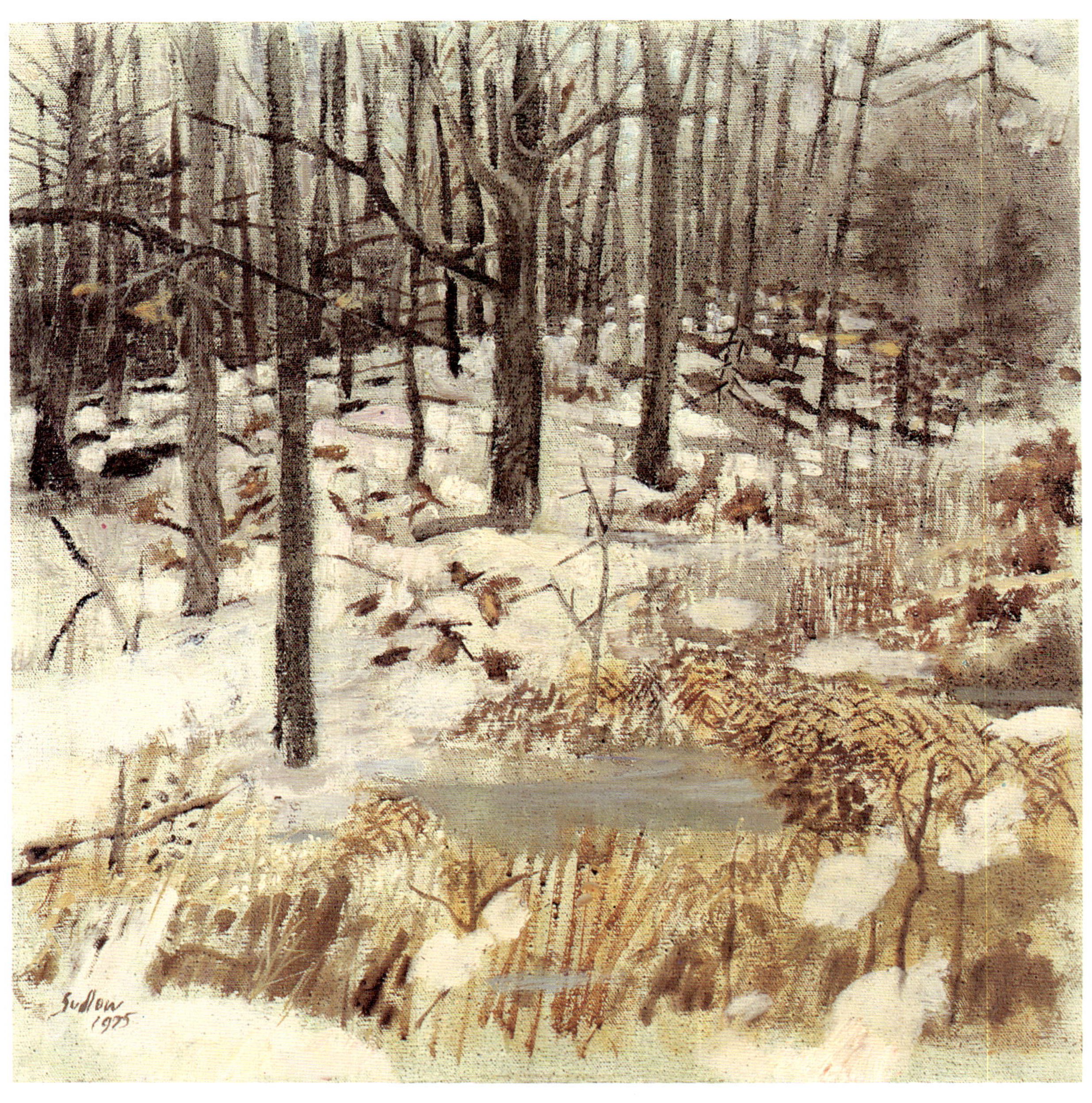

17. *Snow Wood, 1975,* 20″ × 20″
Collection of Mr. & Mrs. Horace Eubank, Topeka, Kansas

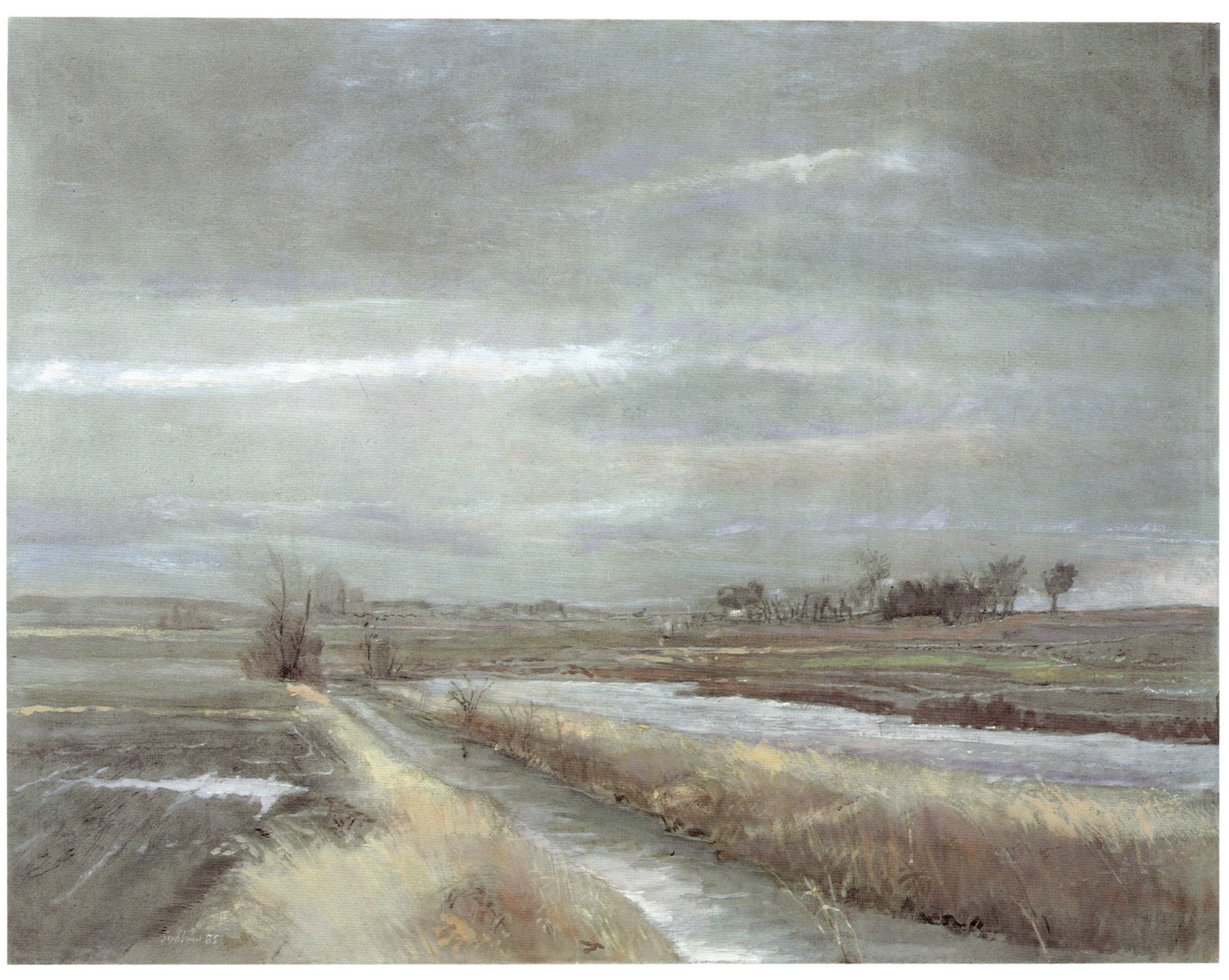

18. *River Flats, 1985,* 40″ × 50″
Collection of Mr. David Wittig, New York, New York

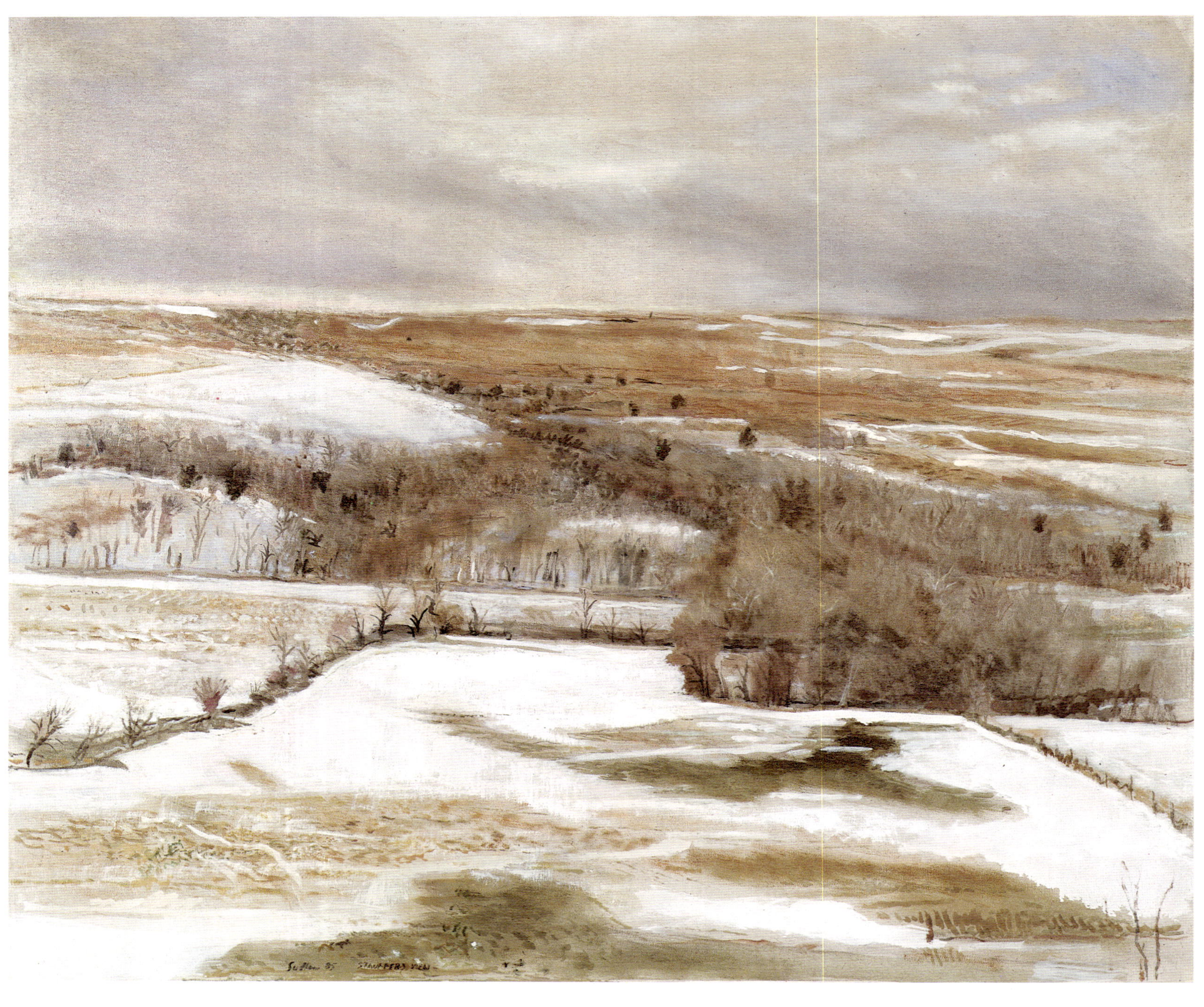

19. *Stauffer's View, 1985,* 42″ × 50″
United Missouri Bancshares, Inc., Kansas City, Missouri

20. *Stull, Winter Stream, 1985,* 50″ × 45″
Collection of Mr. & Mrs. Jerry Moore, Lawrence, Kansas

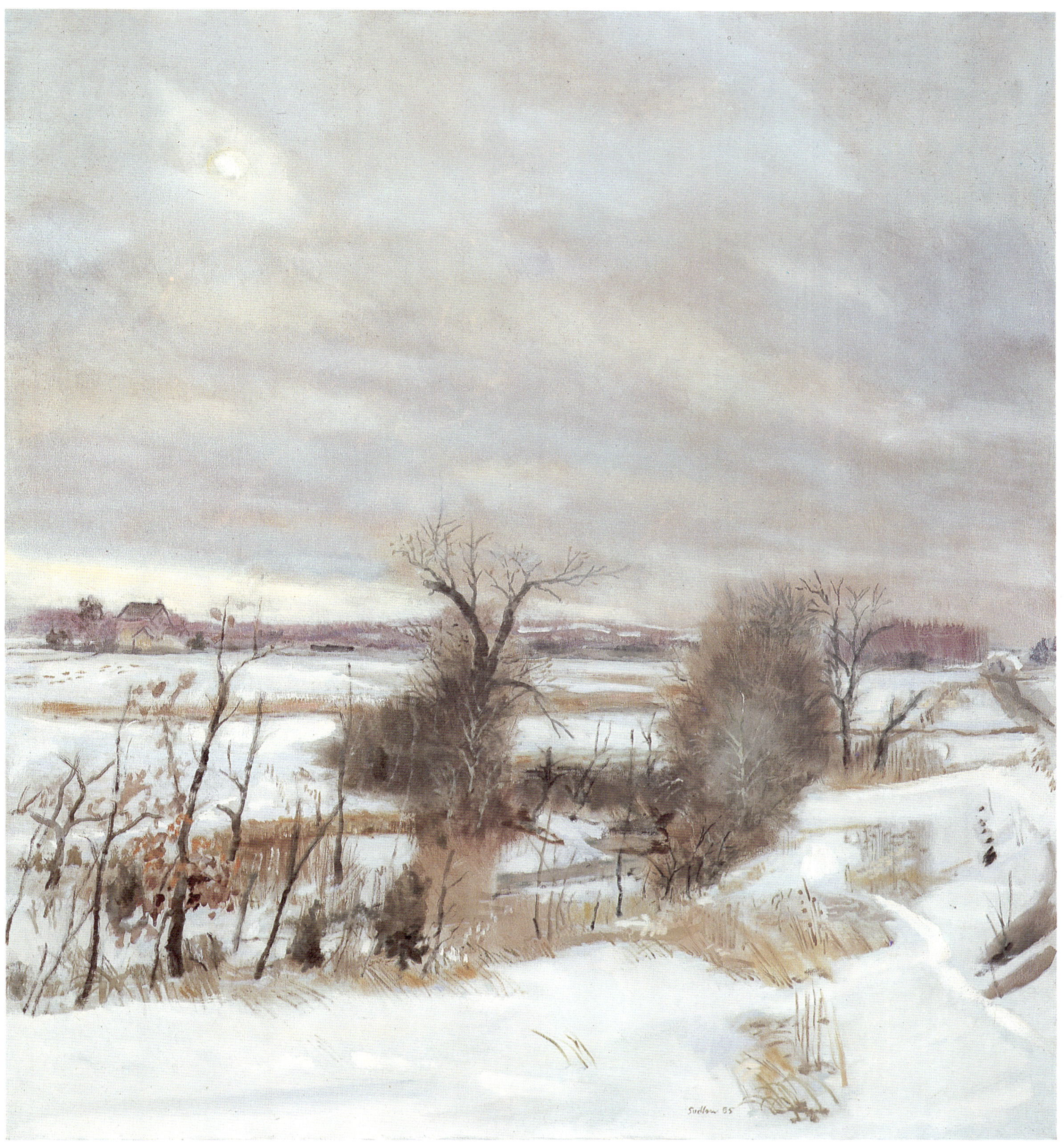
Sudlow 85

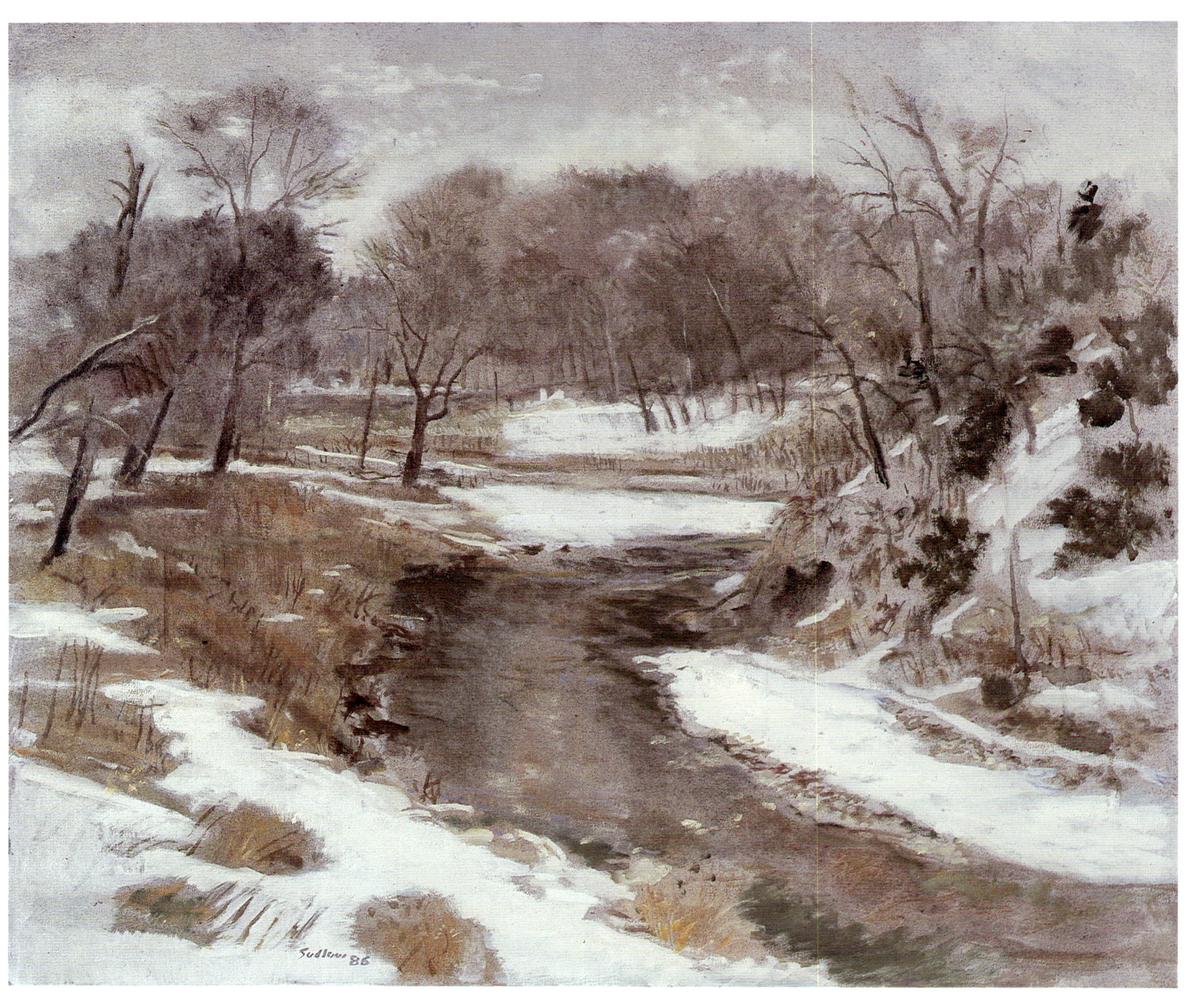

21. *Winter, Mill Creek, 1986,* 34″ × 40″
Beauchamp Frame Shop, Topeka, Kansas

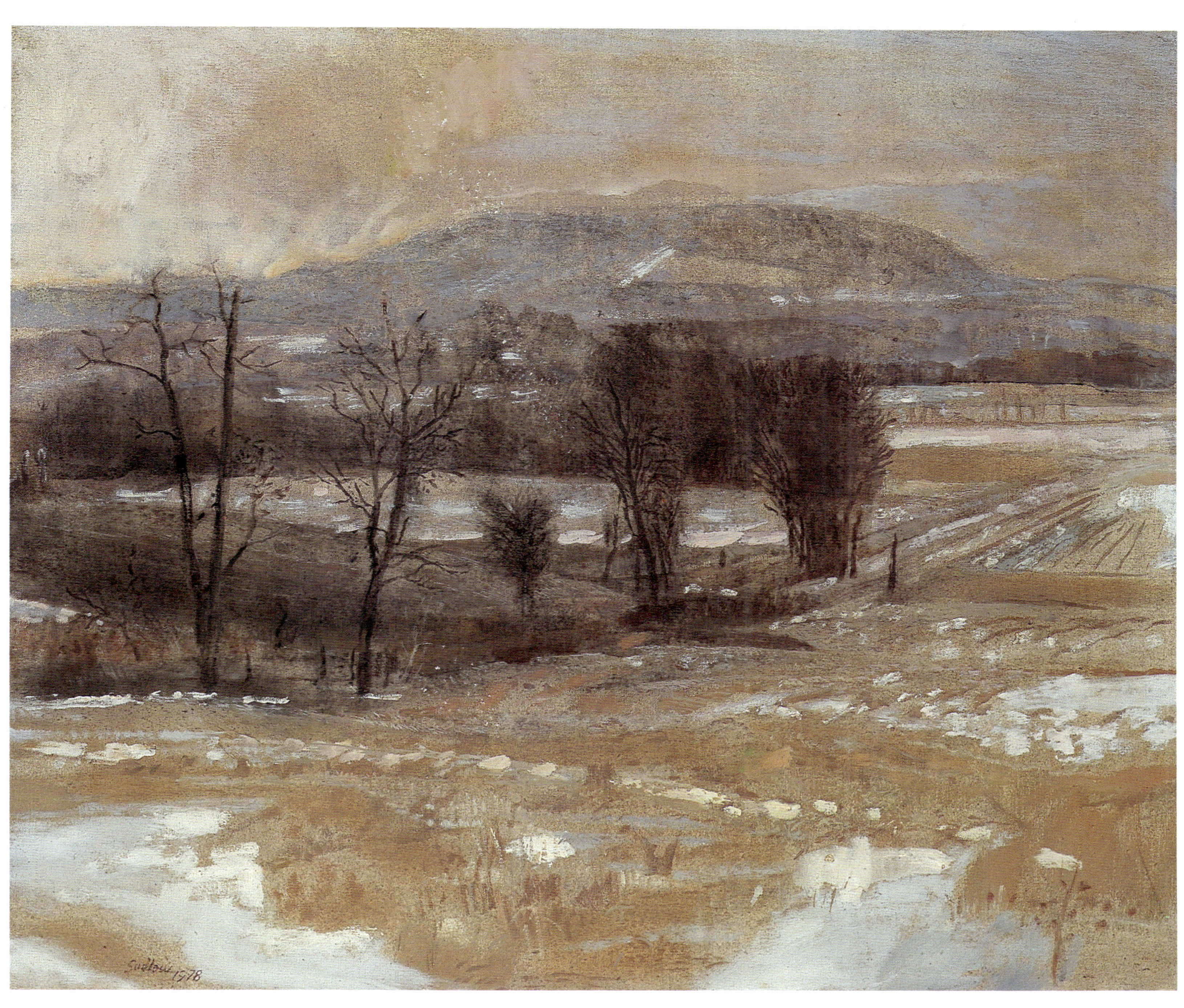

22. *Blue Mound in Snow, 1978,* 24″ × 28″
Collection of Mr. & Mrs. Paul Beauchamp, Topeka, Kansas

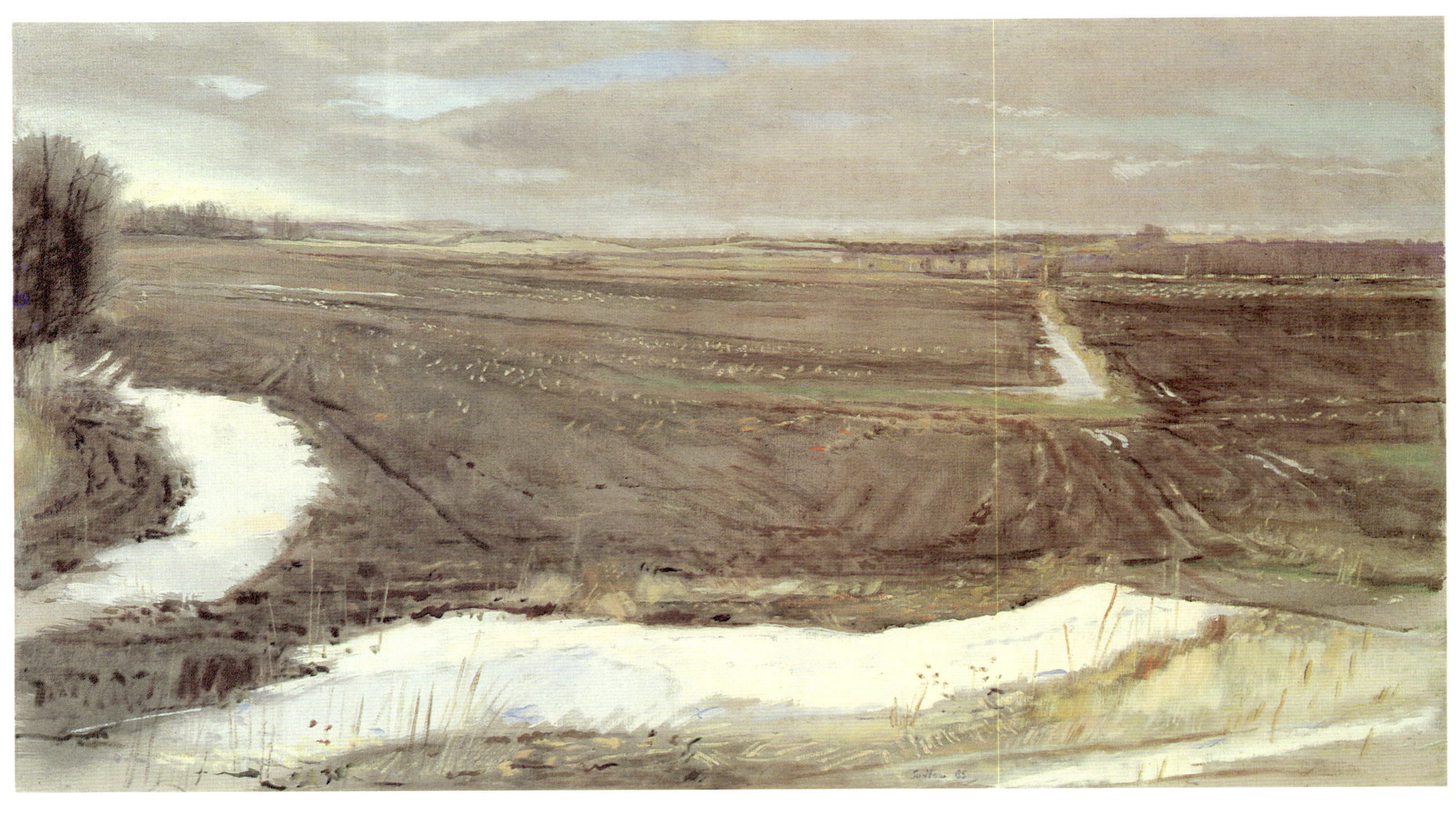

23. *Melting Snow, Wakarusa, 1985,* 28″ × 50″
Beauchamp Frame Shop, Topeka, Kansas

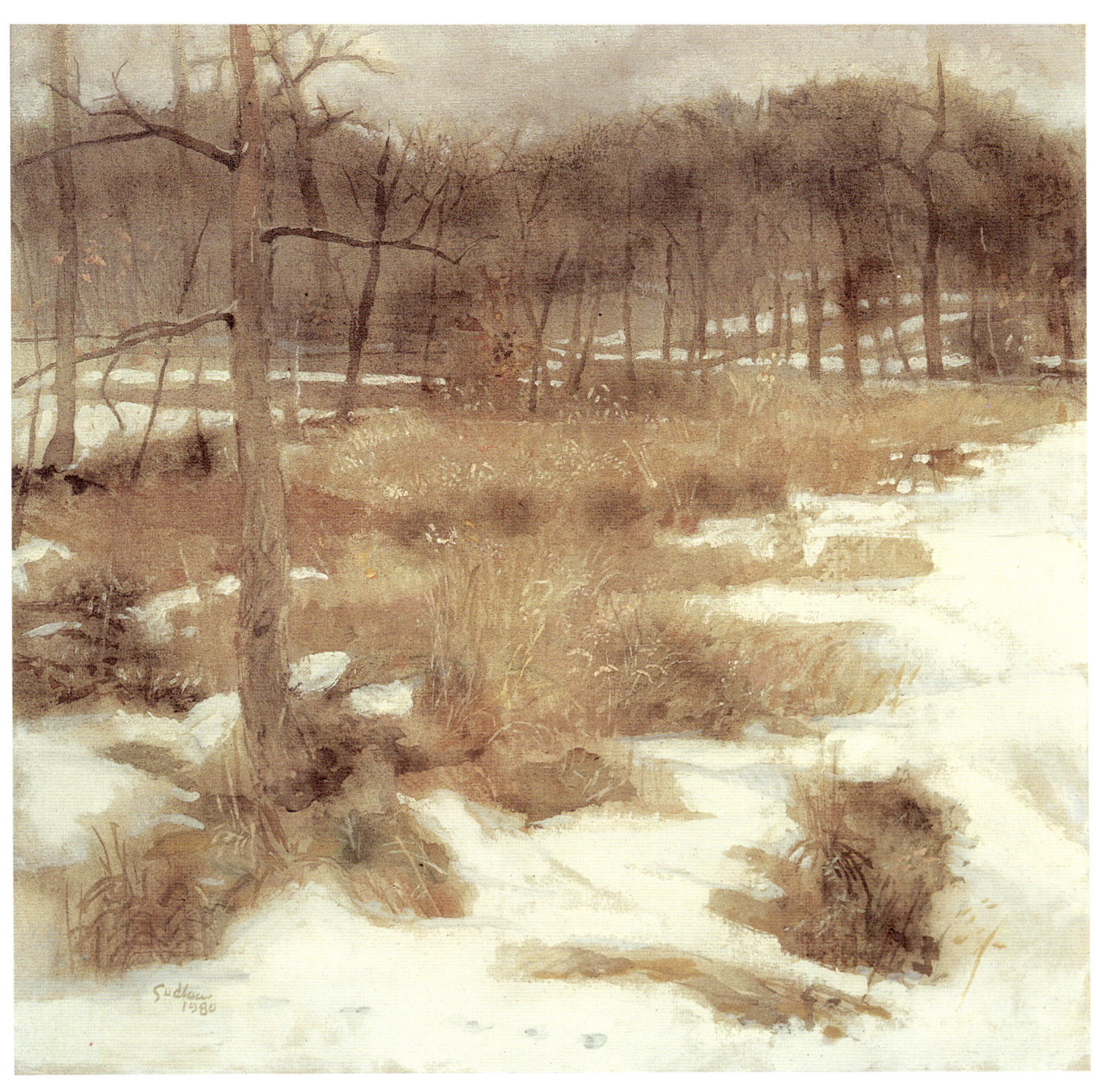

24. *Martin Park Snow, 1980,* 22″ × 22″
Collection of Mr. & Mrs. Paul Beauchamp, Topeka, Kansas

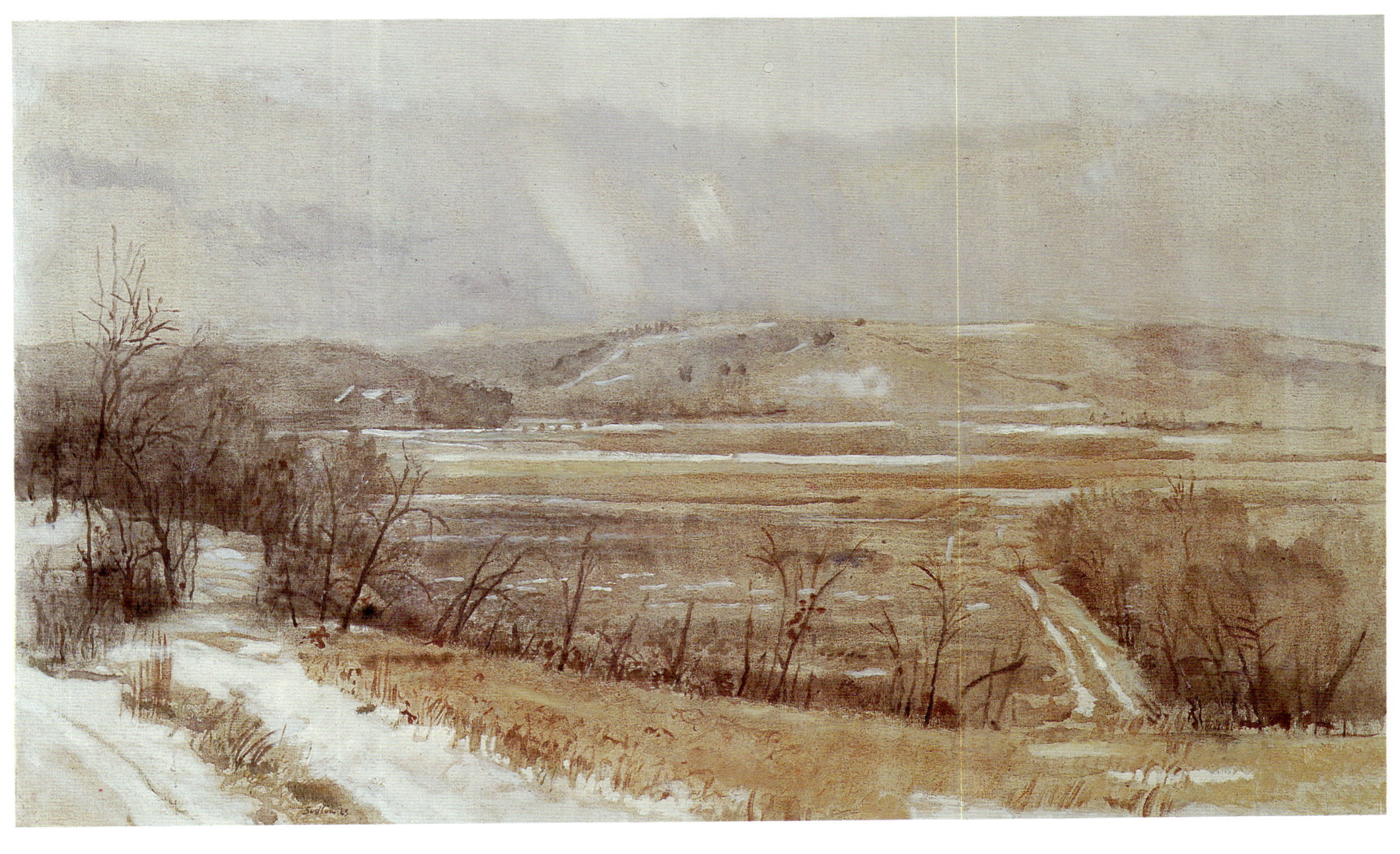

25. *Chicken Creek Whiteout, 1985,* 28″ × 46″
Canaan Farm, Tonganoxie, Kansas

26. *Snowfield South of Stull, 1986,* 42″ × 42″
Canaan Farm, Tonganoxie, Kansas

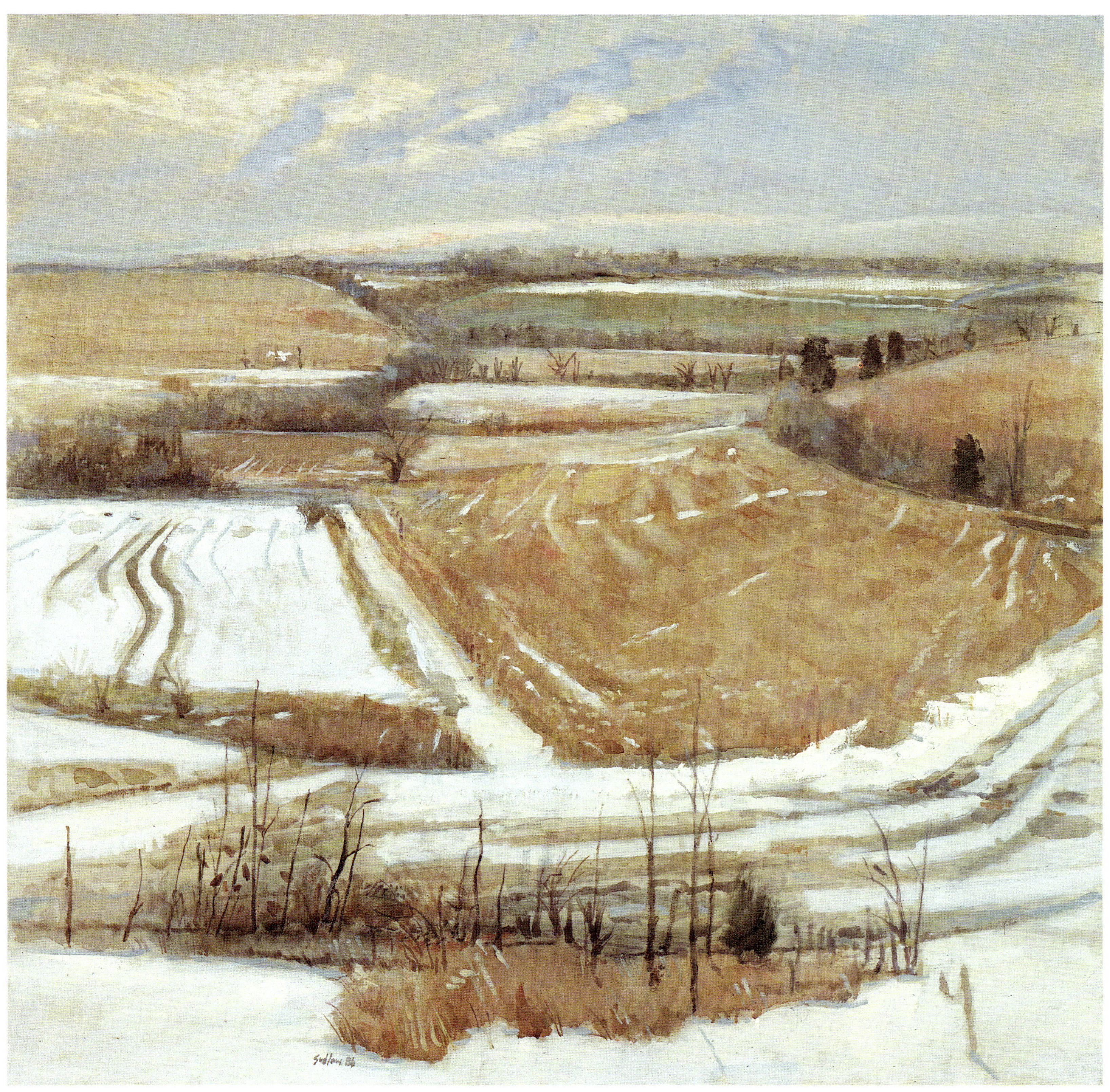

Spring and Summer

The season outruns me. Already flowers turn to fruit, seeds form, the chick is in the egg, yet I remember bare twigs and ice. My palette is stuck in winter's sparseness.

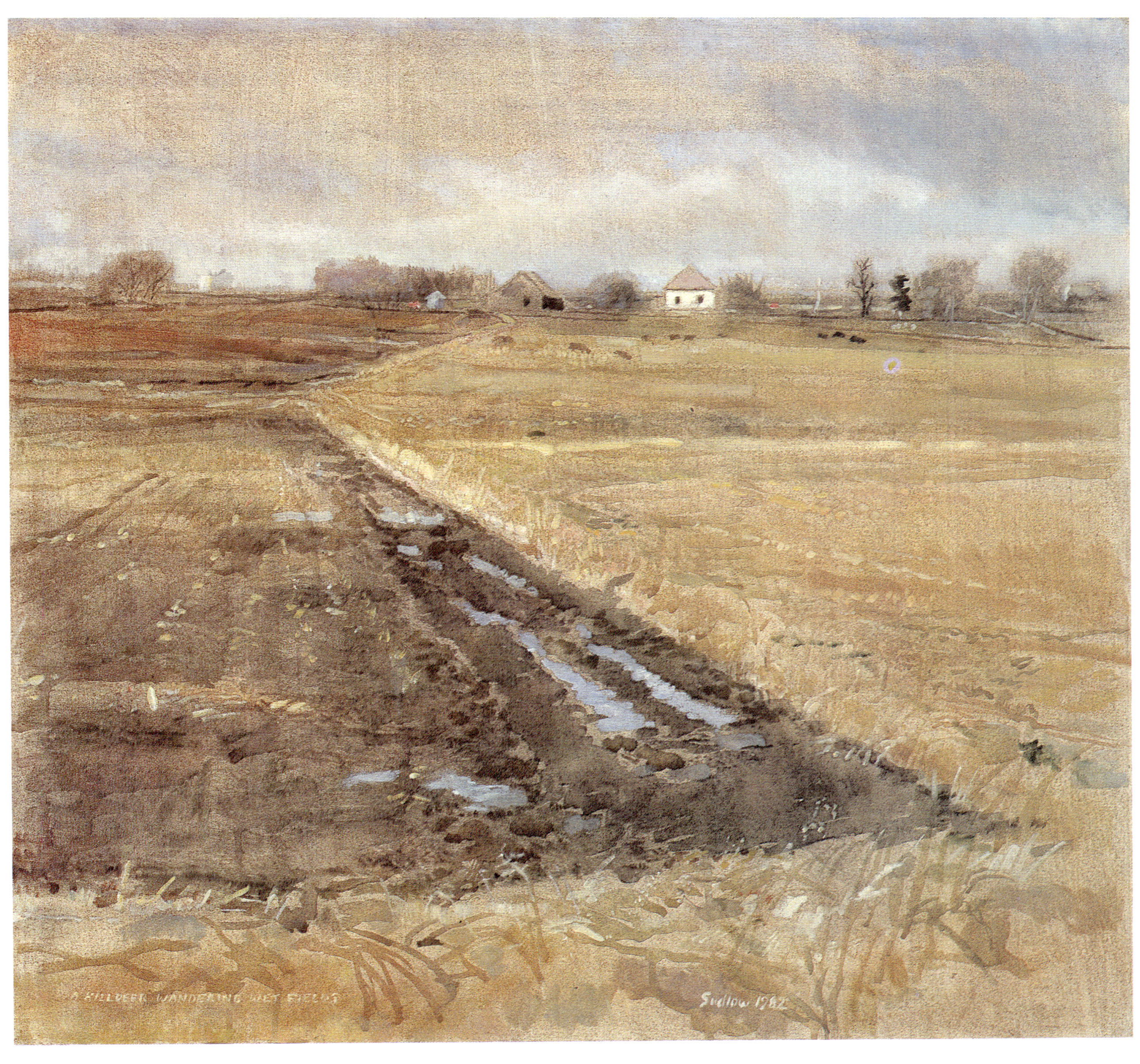

27. *Killdeer Wandering Wet Fields, 1982,* 30″ × 31″
Private Collection

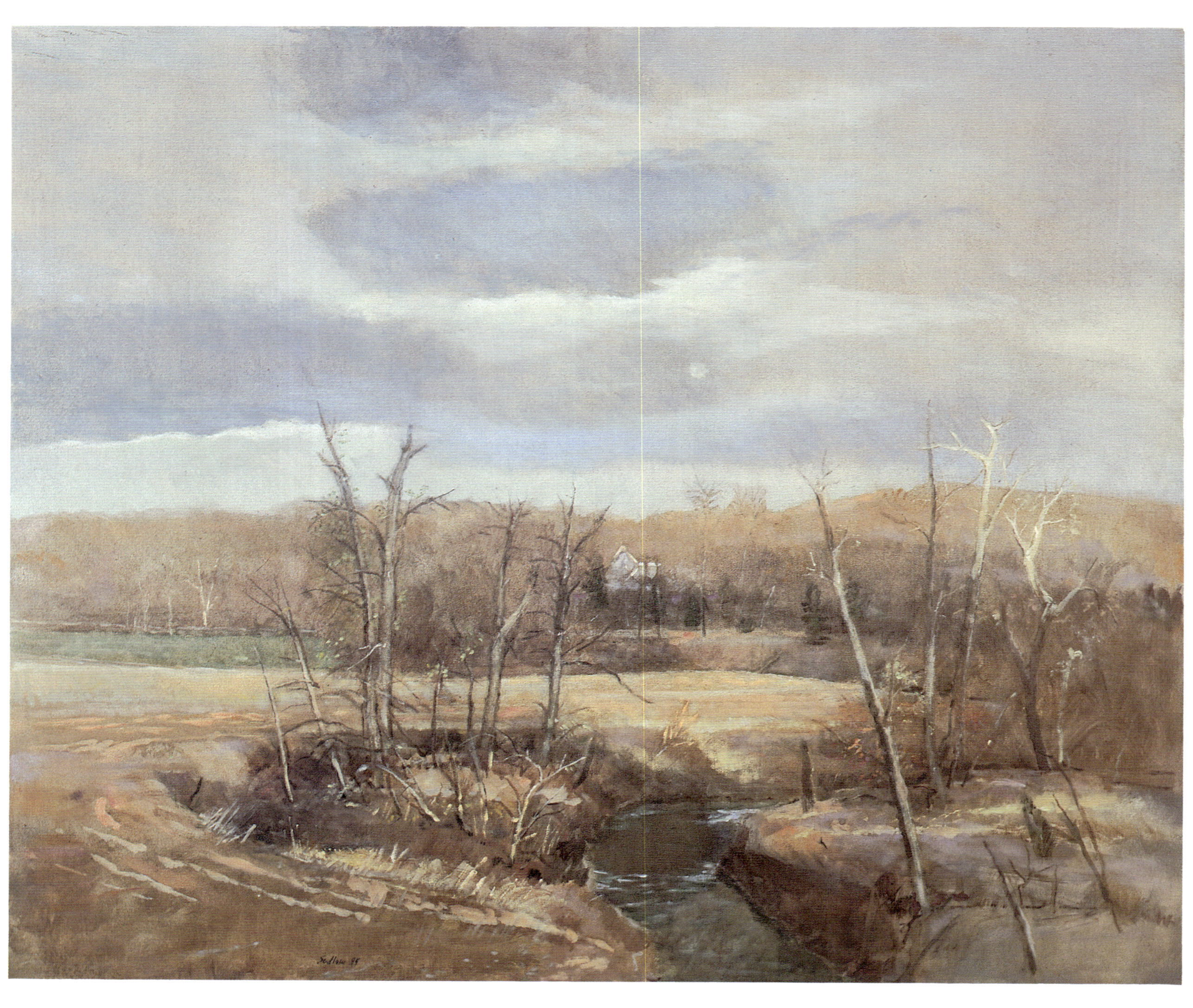

28. *Early Spring, Chicken Creek, 1985,* 42″ × 50″
Collection of Mr. & Mrs. Lee Capps, Lawrence, Kansas

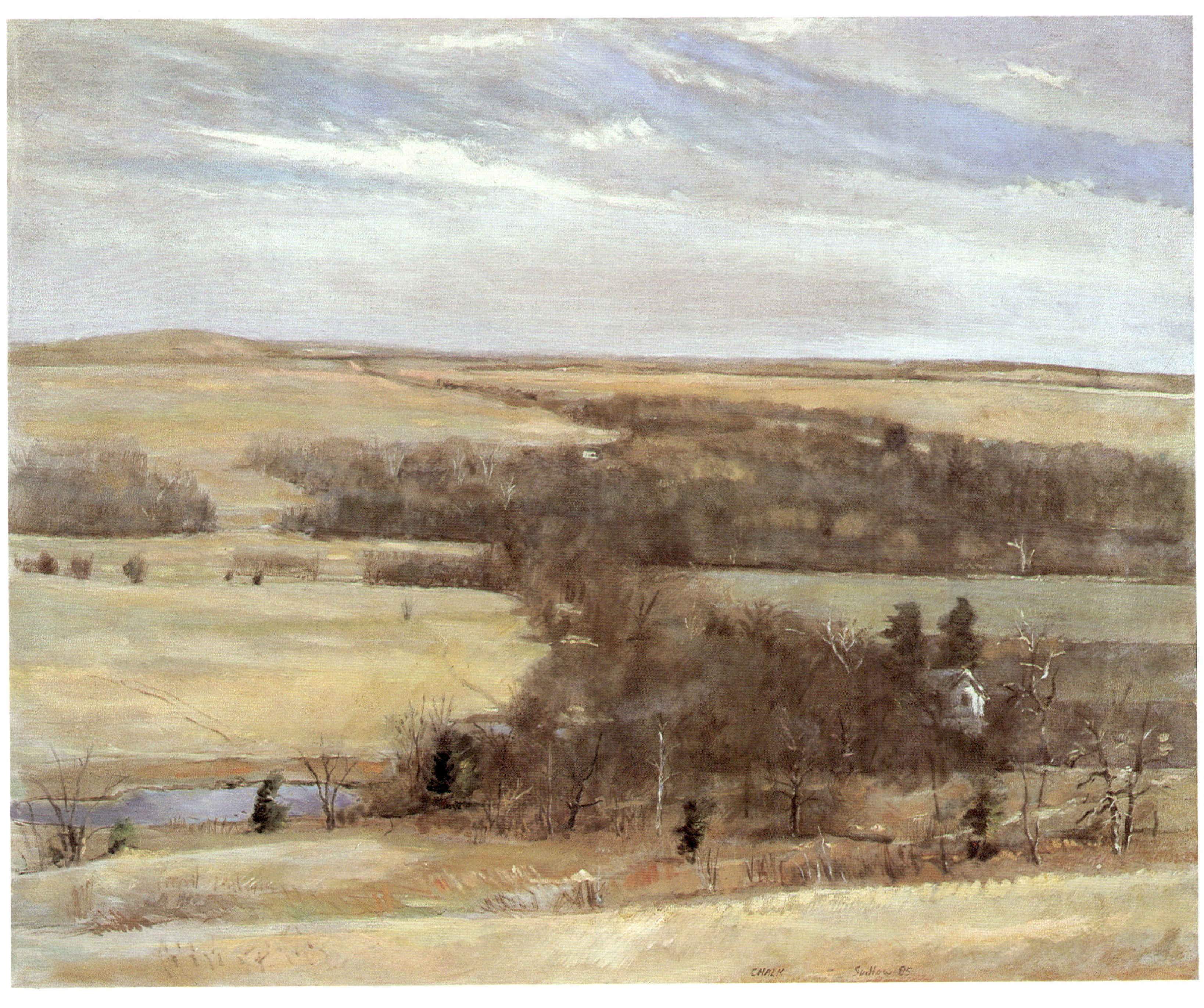

29. *Windy Spring Sky, Chalk, 1985,* 42″ × 50″
The Carter Waters Corporation, Kansas City, Missouri

Tonight canopies of clouds throb with the infections of storm. The flashes of lightning appear as livid inflammation, pain and anguish seem to tear the dark landscape, and birds flutter in fear. Beyond all this local turbulence the upper sky is serene and undisturbed.

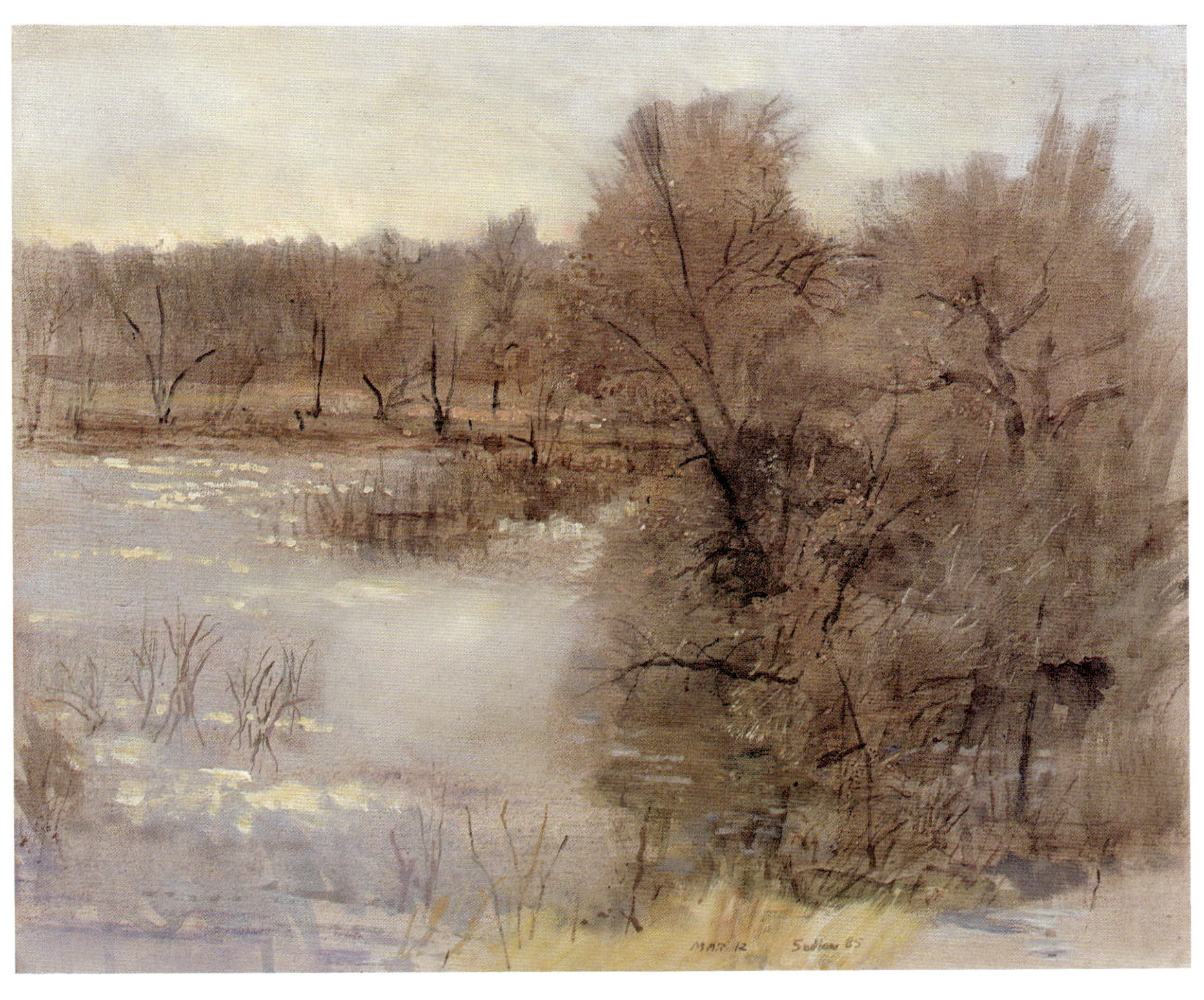

30. *Frog Song Pond, 1985,* 20″ × 24″
Collection of Mr. & Mrs. Ron Olsen, Lawrence, Kansas

31. *Overbrook Triptych, 1984,* 40″ × 80″
Hallmark Cards, Inc., Lawrence, Kansas

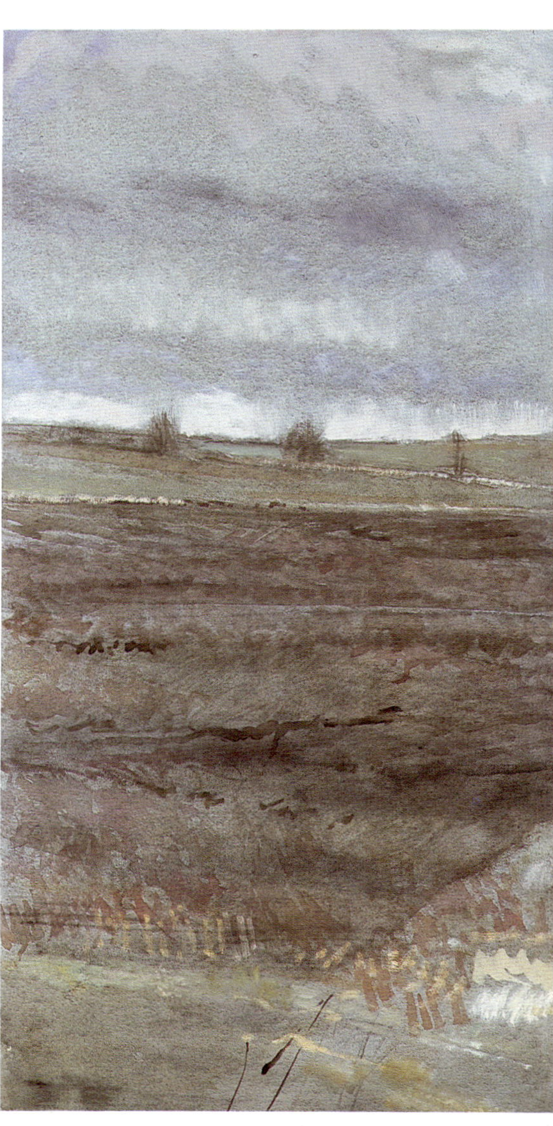

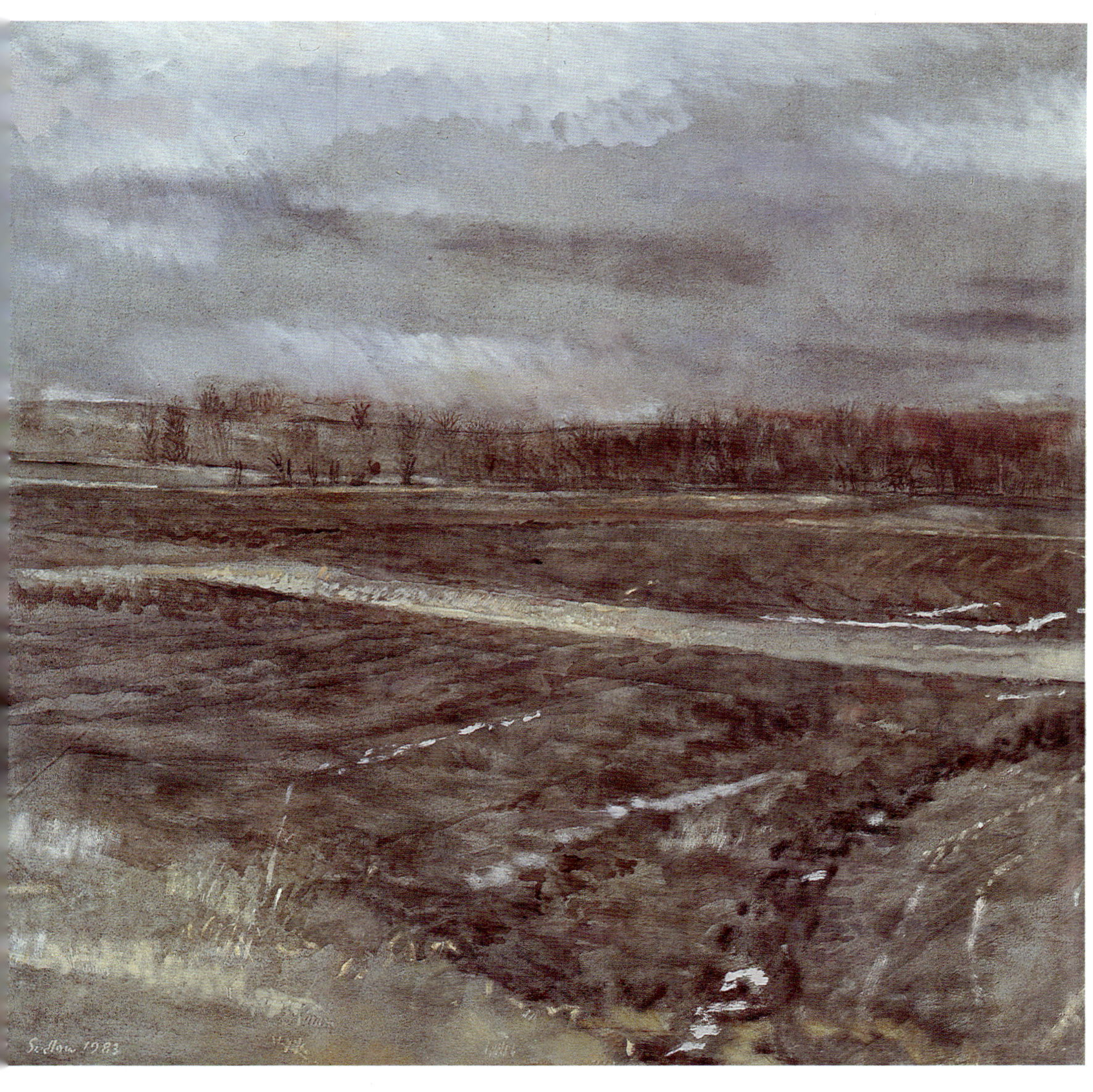
Sudlow 1983

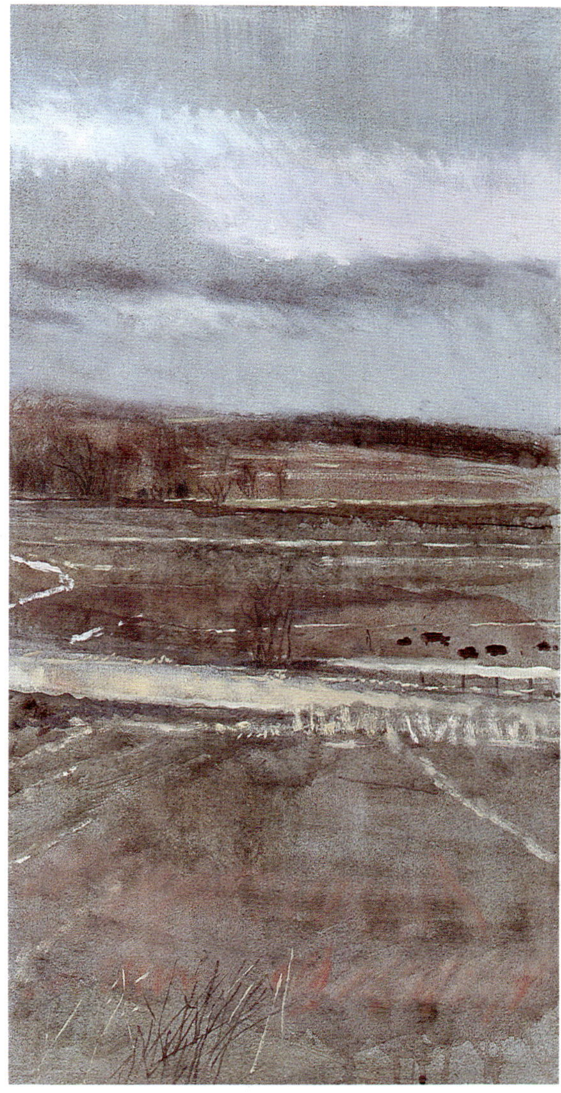

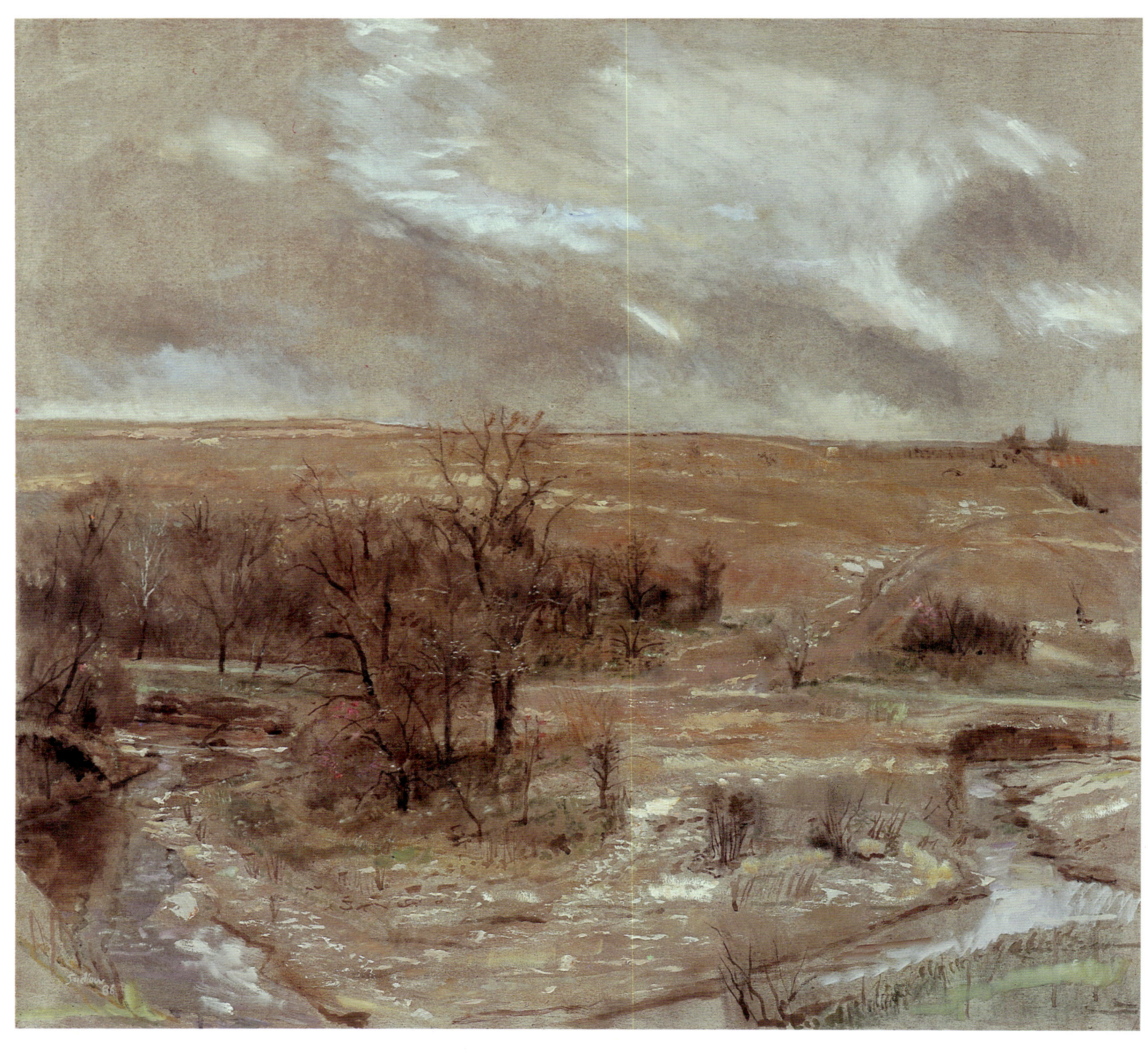

32. *Bursting Spring, Flint Hills, 1986*, 44″ × 48″
Artist's Collection

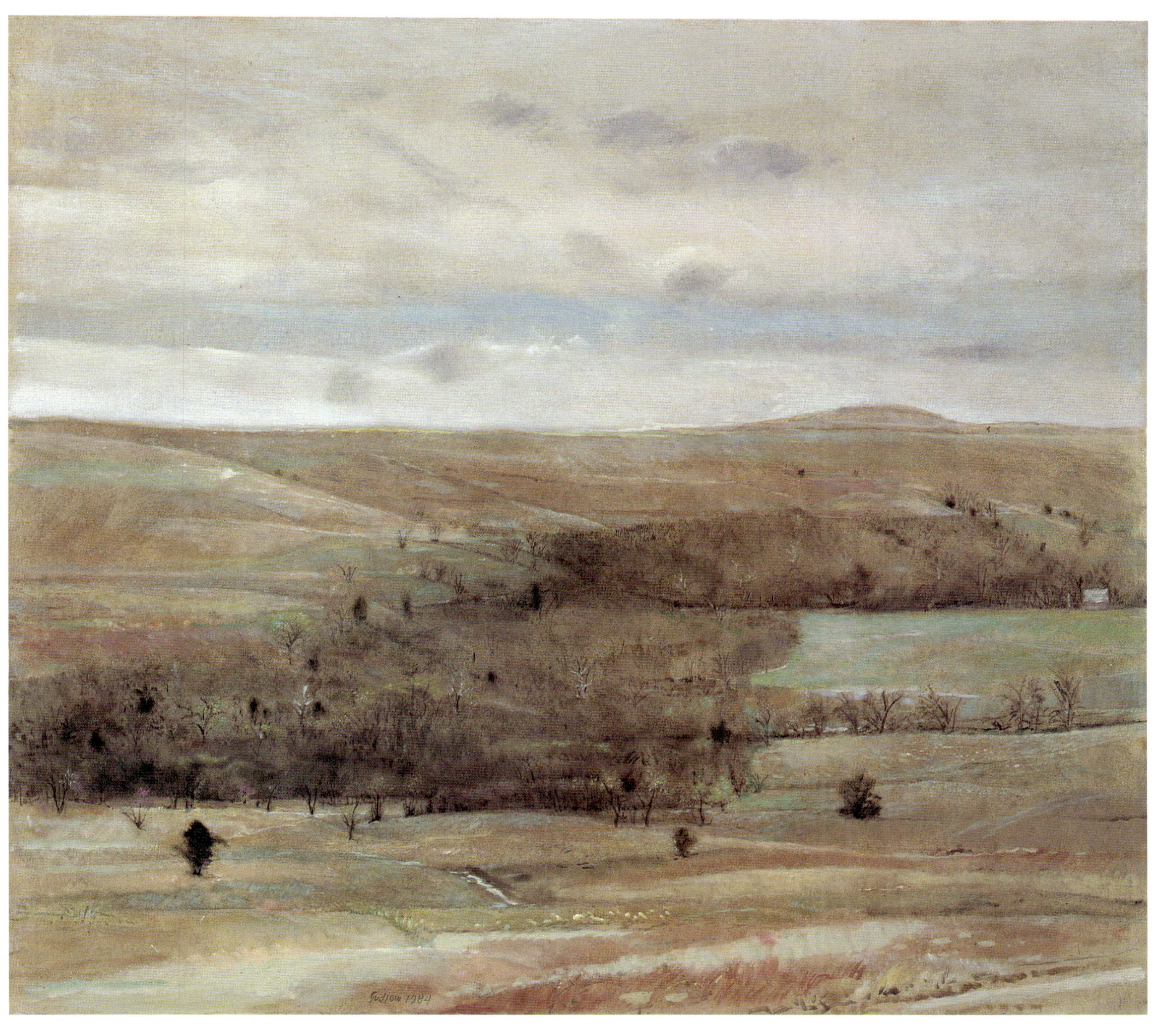

33. *West of Alma, 1984,* 45″ × 50″
Artist's Collection

34. *Pioneer Bluffs, Spring, 1986,* 48″ × 44″
Artist's Collection

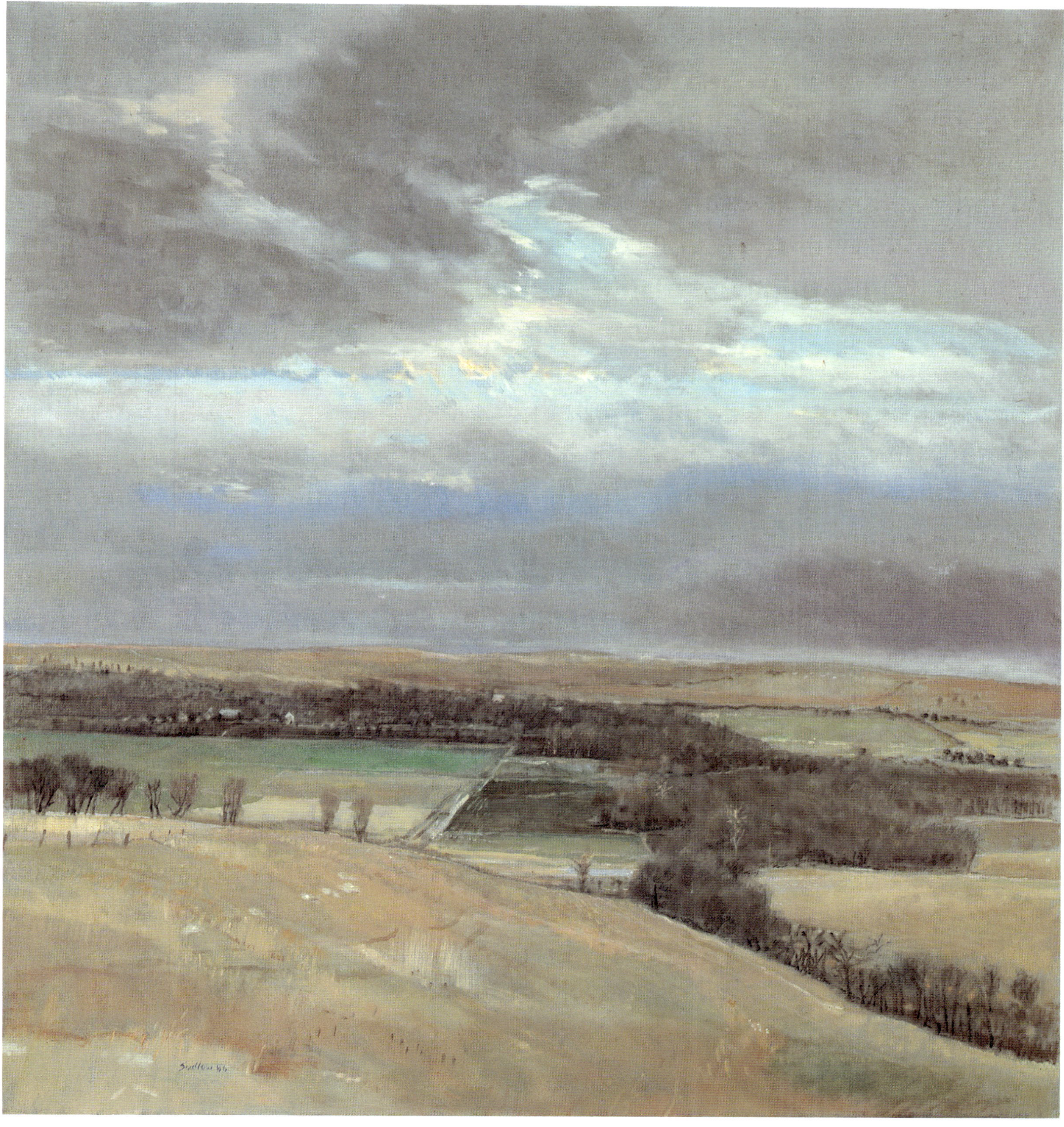

A sudden, great, golden sky with a molten, plunging sun blazing through shelves of incandescent clouds. All this is performed in solemn silence.

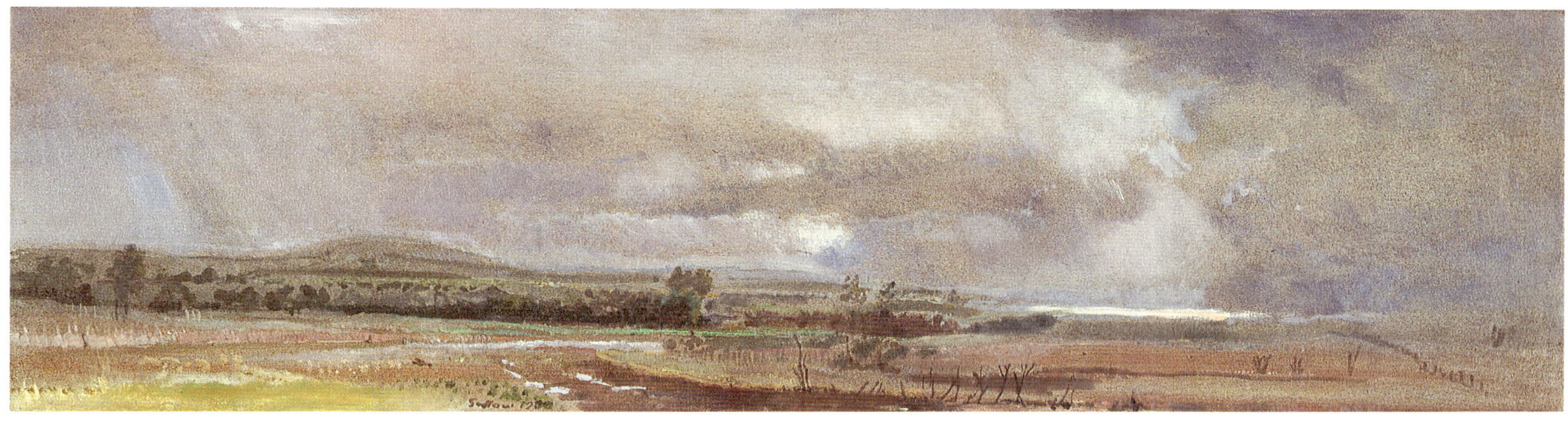

35. *Rainstorm, Flint Hills, 1982, 11″ × 40″*
Collection of Mr. & Mrs. David Zacharias, Topeka, Kansas

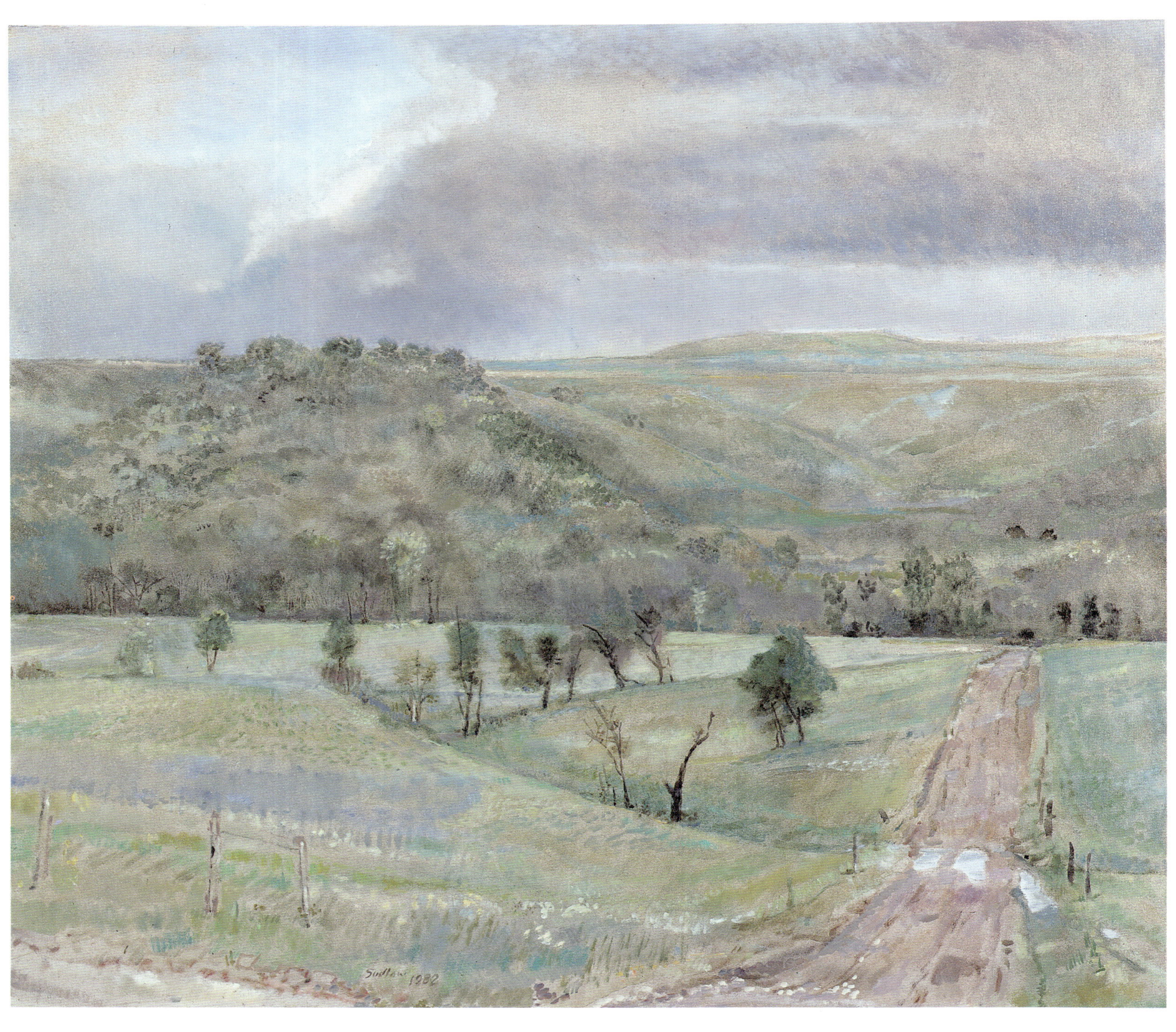

36. *After the Rain, Flint Hills, 1981,* 45″ × 50″
Private Collection

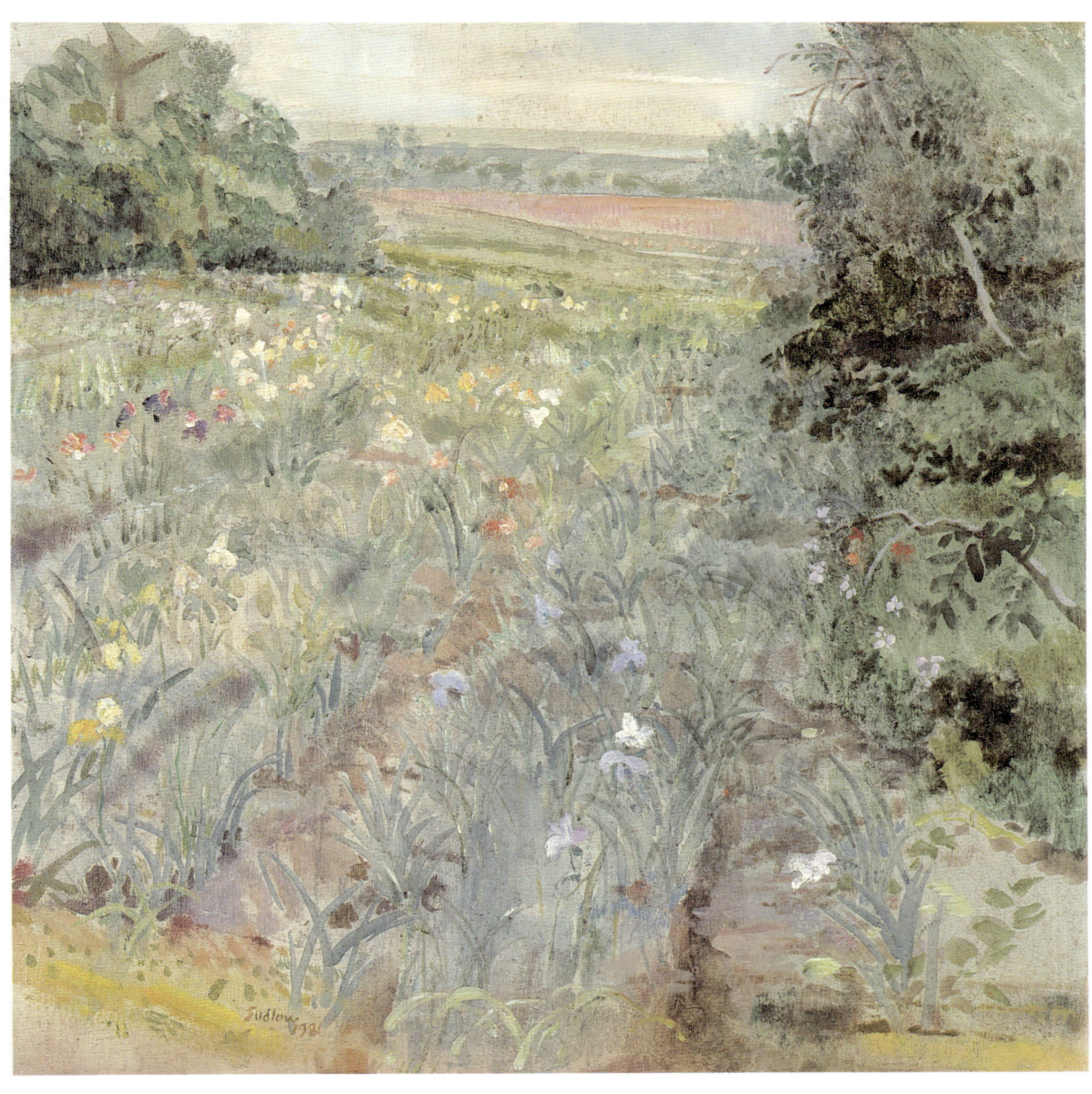

37. *Iris Garden, 1981,* 24″ × 24″
Canaan Farm, Tonganoxie, Kansas

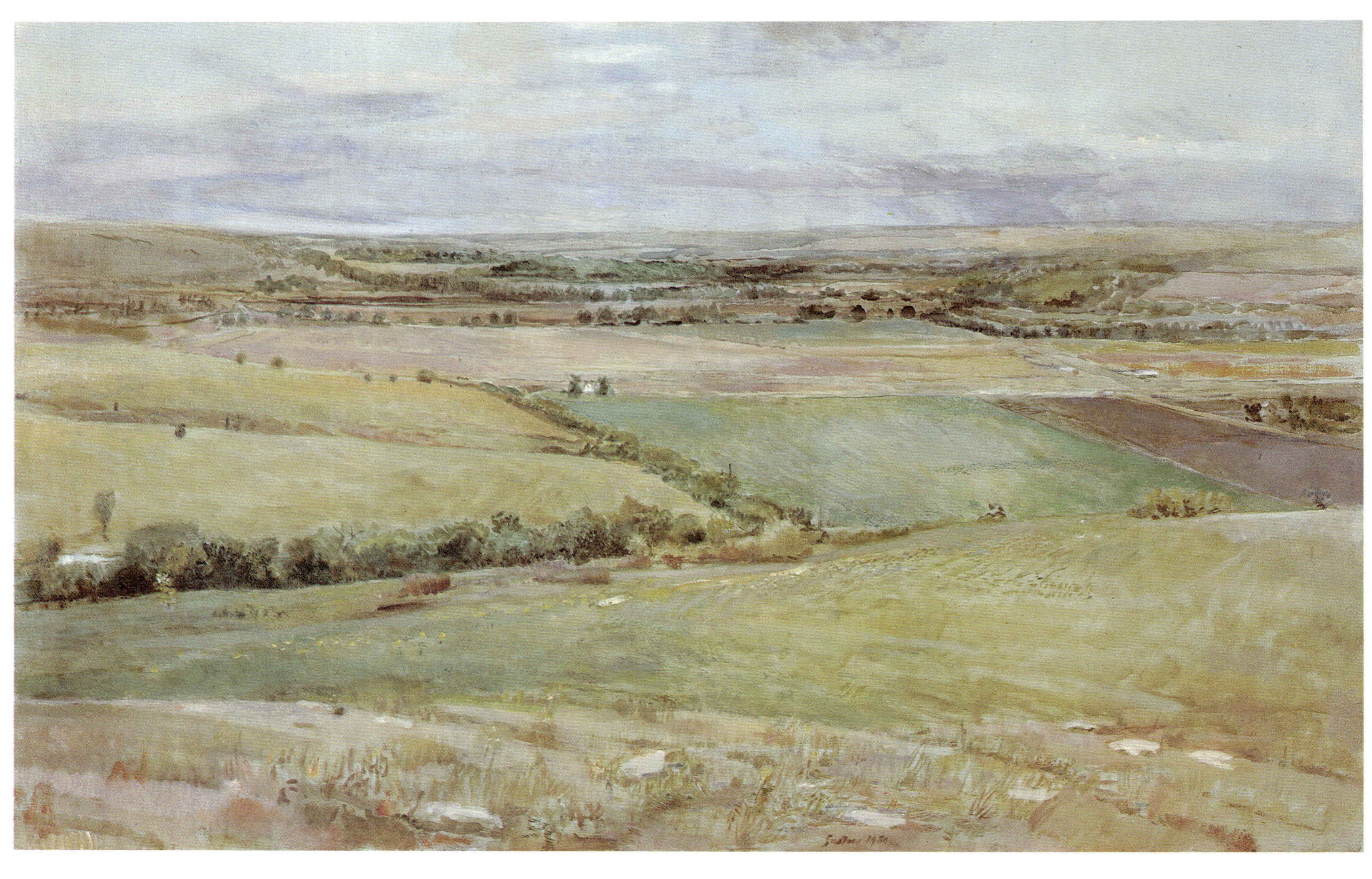

38. *From Buffalo Mound, 1980,* 38″ × 48″
Private Collection

39. *Mill Creek Glade, 1985,* 50″ × 43″
American Legacy Gallery, Kansas City, Missouri

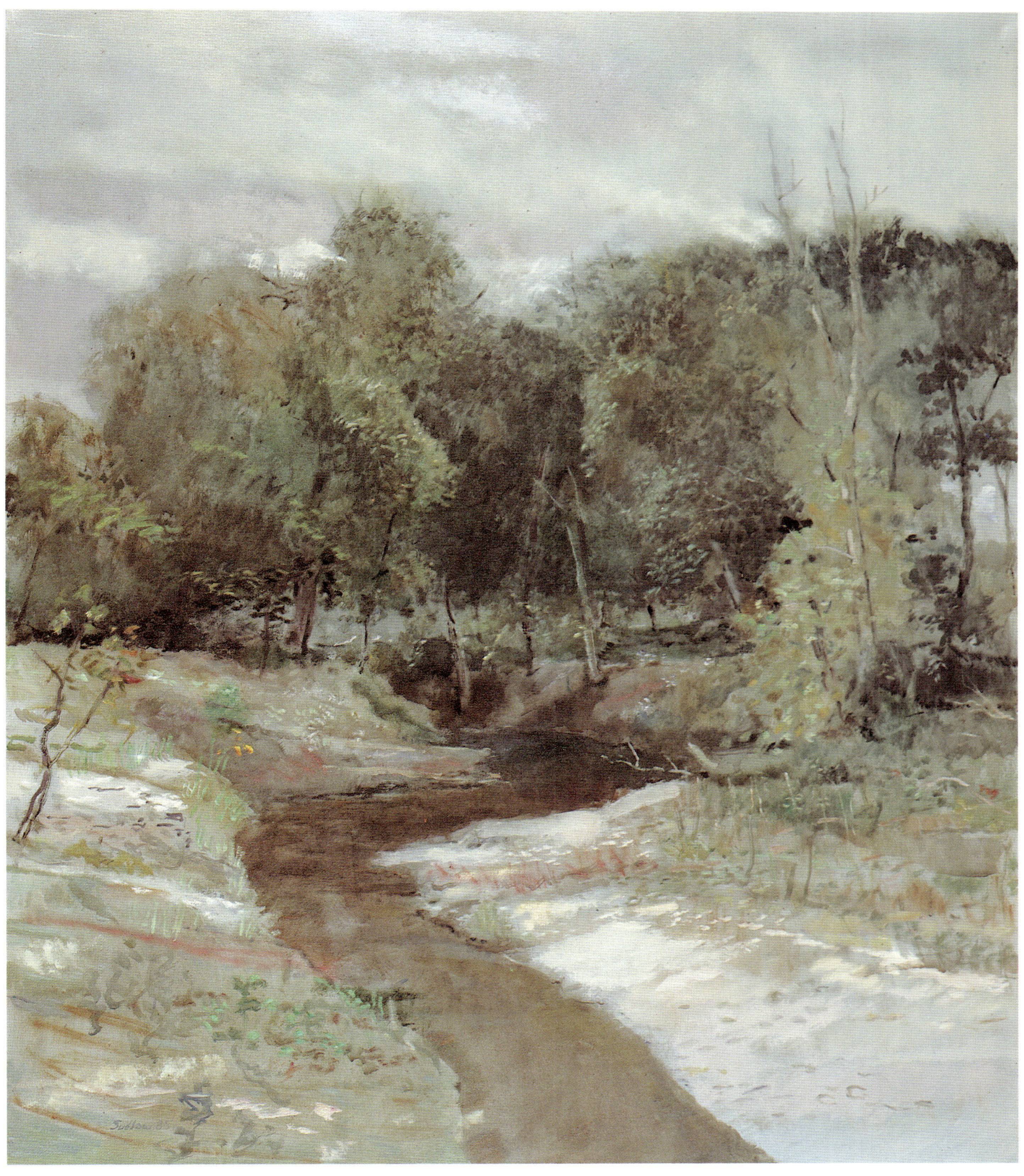

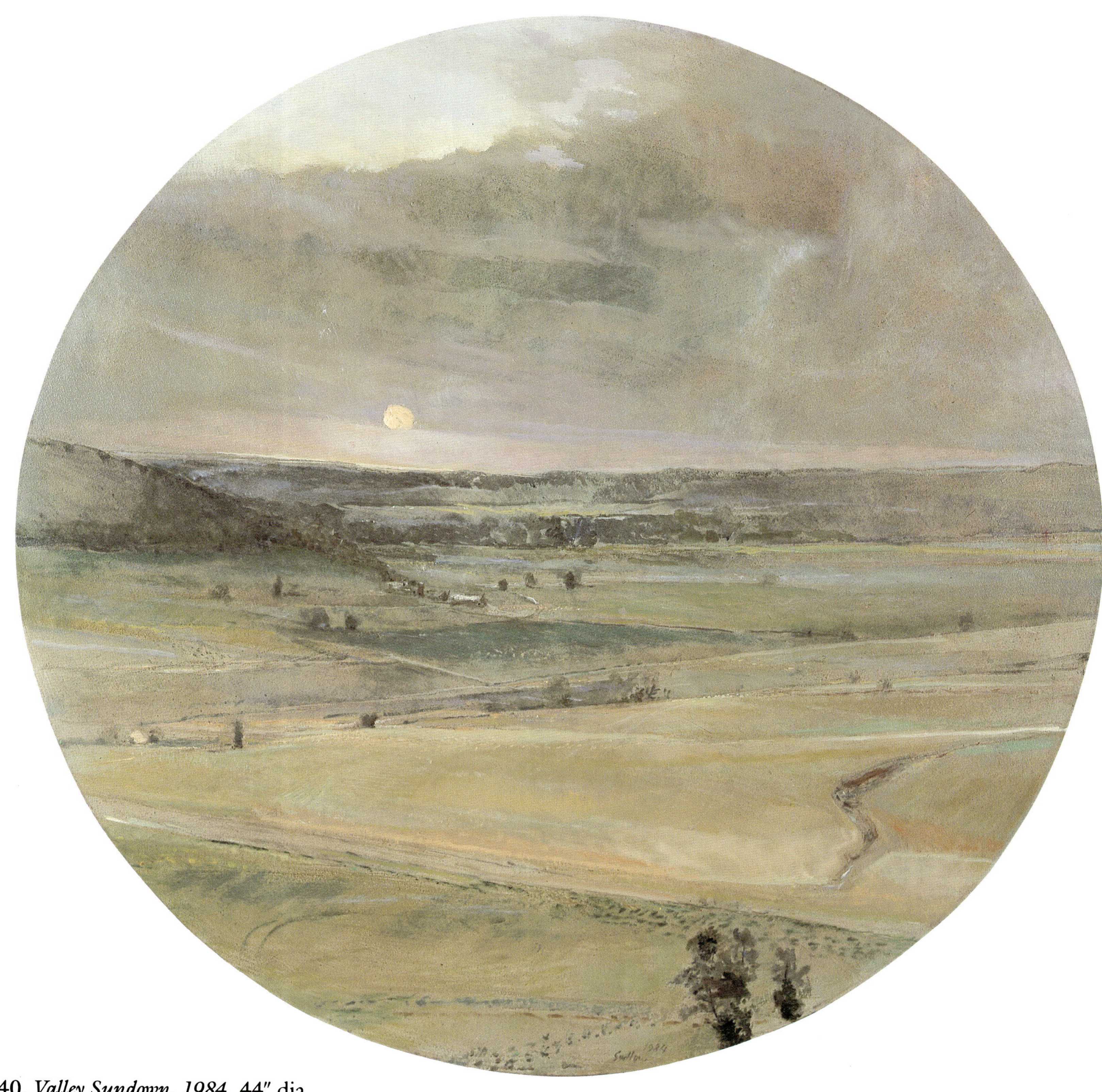

40. *Valley Sundown, 1984,* 44″ dia.
Artist's Collection

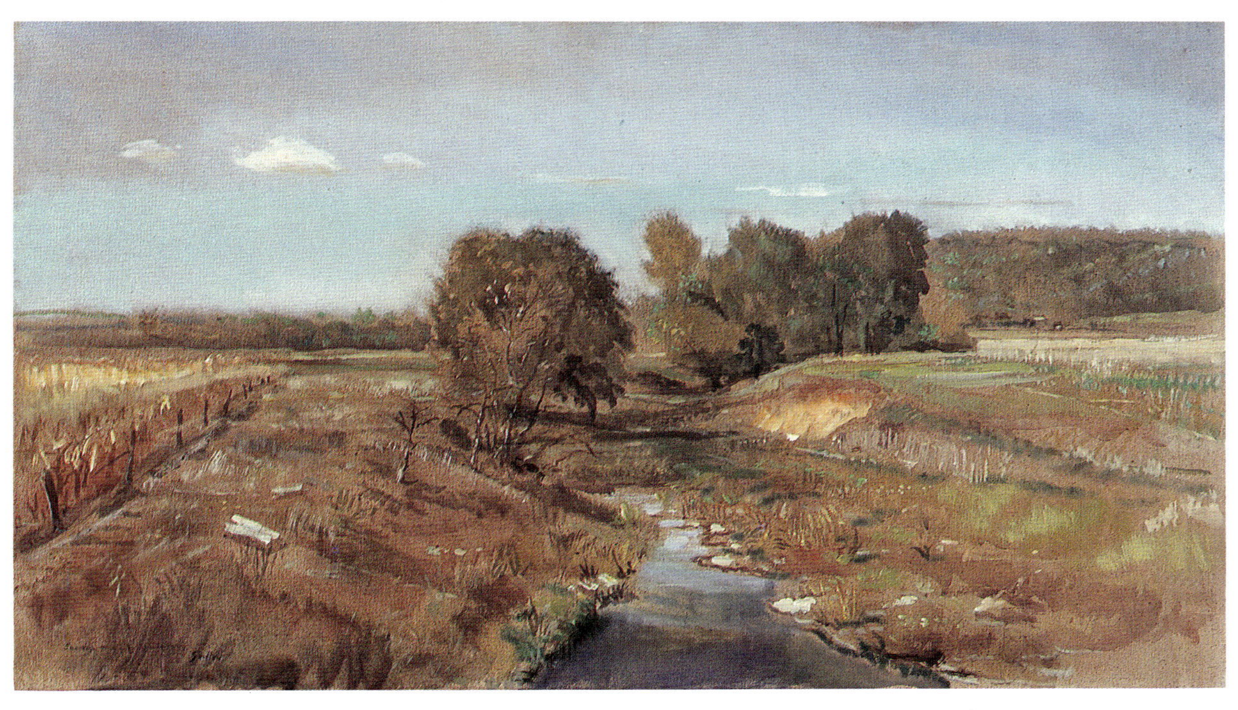

41. *Sunday Morning, 1984,* 22″ × 35″
Collection of Mrs. Guy V. Keeler, Lawrence, Kansas

Fall

From a scanning eye the whole ensemble, sky, earth, and sunlight are caught in fusion. Nothing is seen in isolation; all things are a part of the whole. The landscape is a living entity, never still or fixed. This is the world I encounter, a paradox I would paint.

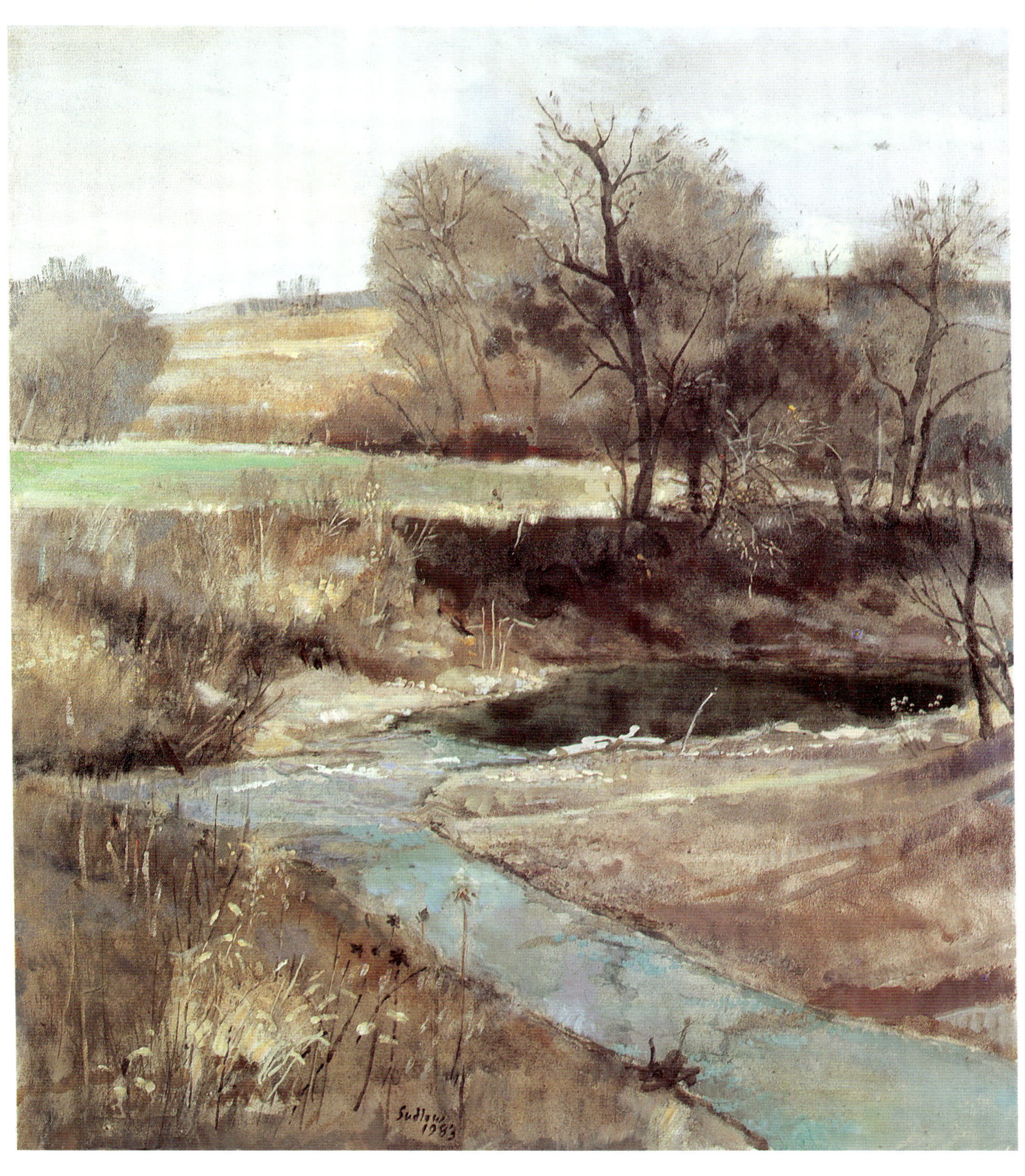

42. *Mill Creek, 1982, 26″ × 22″*
Private Collection

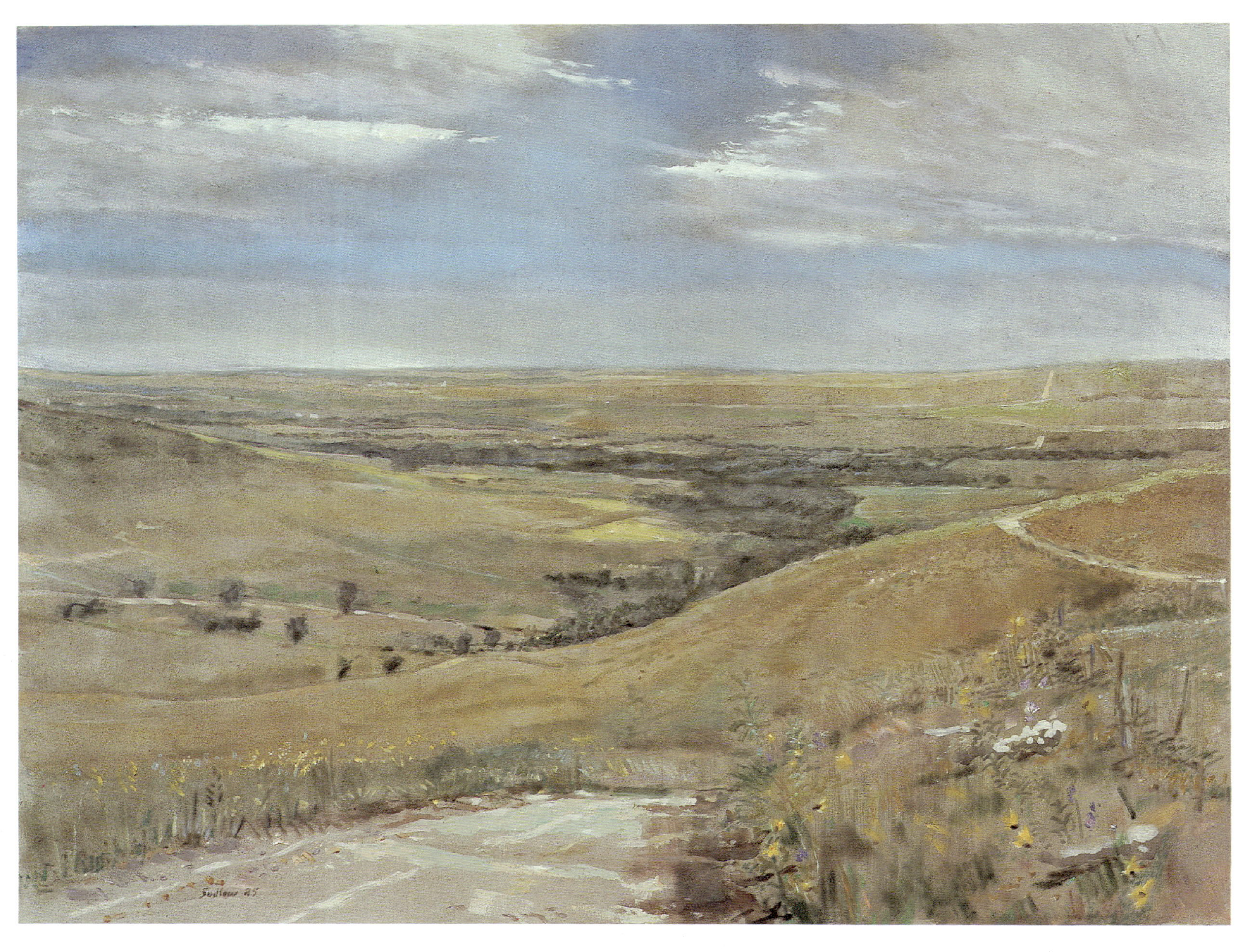

43. *Early Fall, Mill Creek Valley, 1985,* 38″ × 50″
Collection of Mr. & Mrs. William Shackelford, Shawnee Mission, Kansas

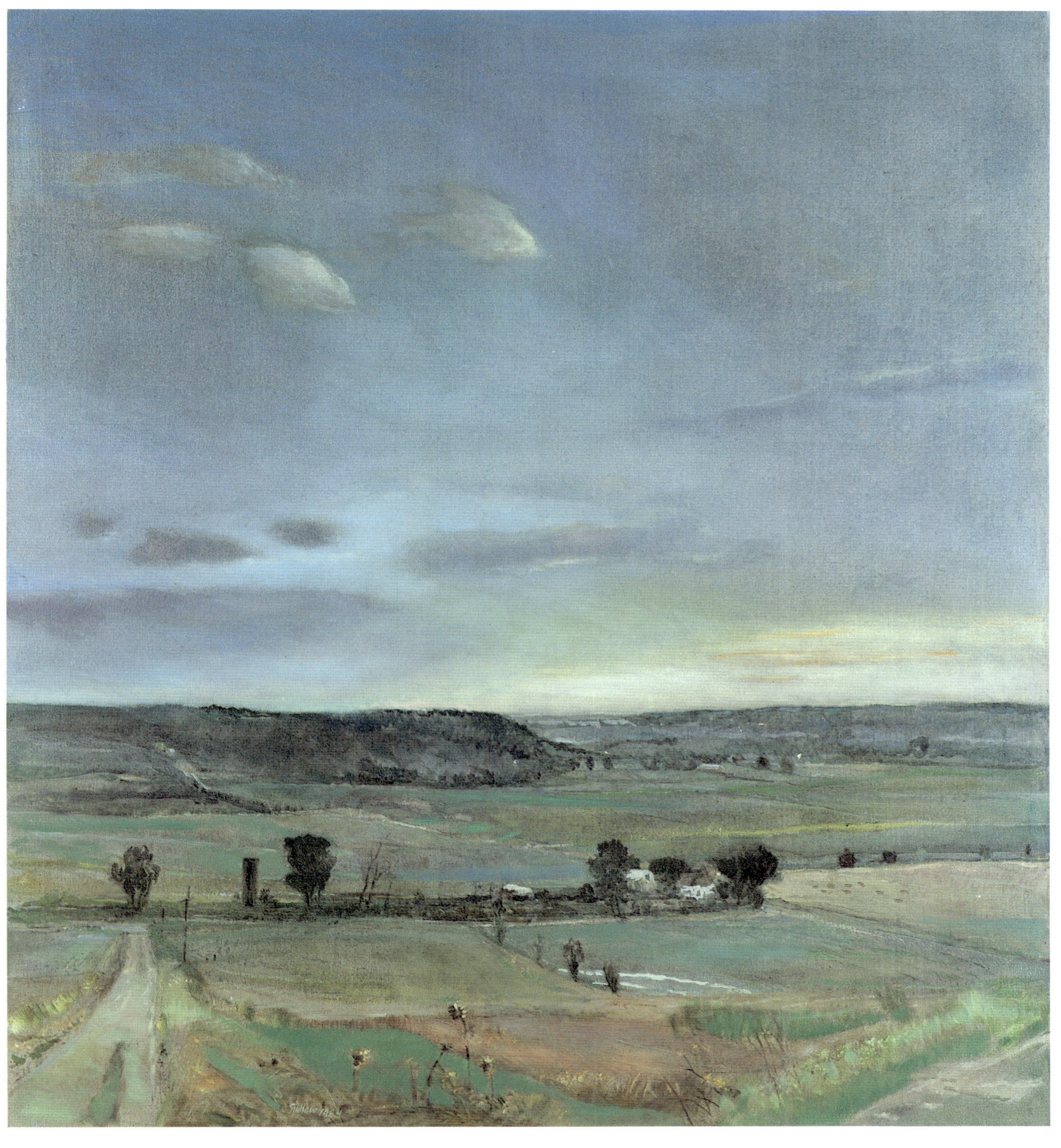

44. *Markley Sundown, 1985,* 50″ × 45″
American Legacy Gallery, Kansas City, Missouri

The rain scatters a flight of blackbirds. Silvery streaks gash across the old grain field and a sudden wet wind sweeps the grasses double. The horizon dissolves and in an instant all my patterns go asunder.

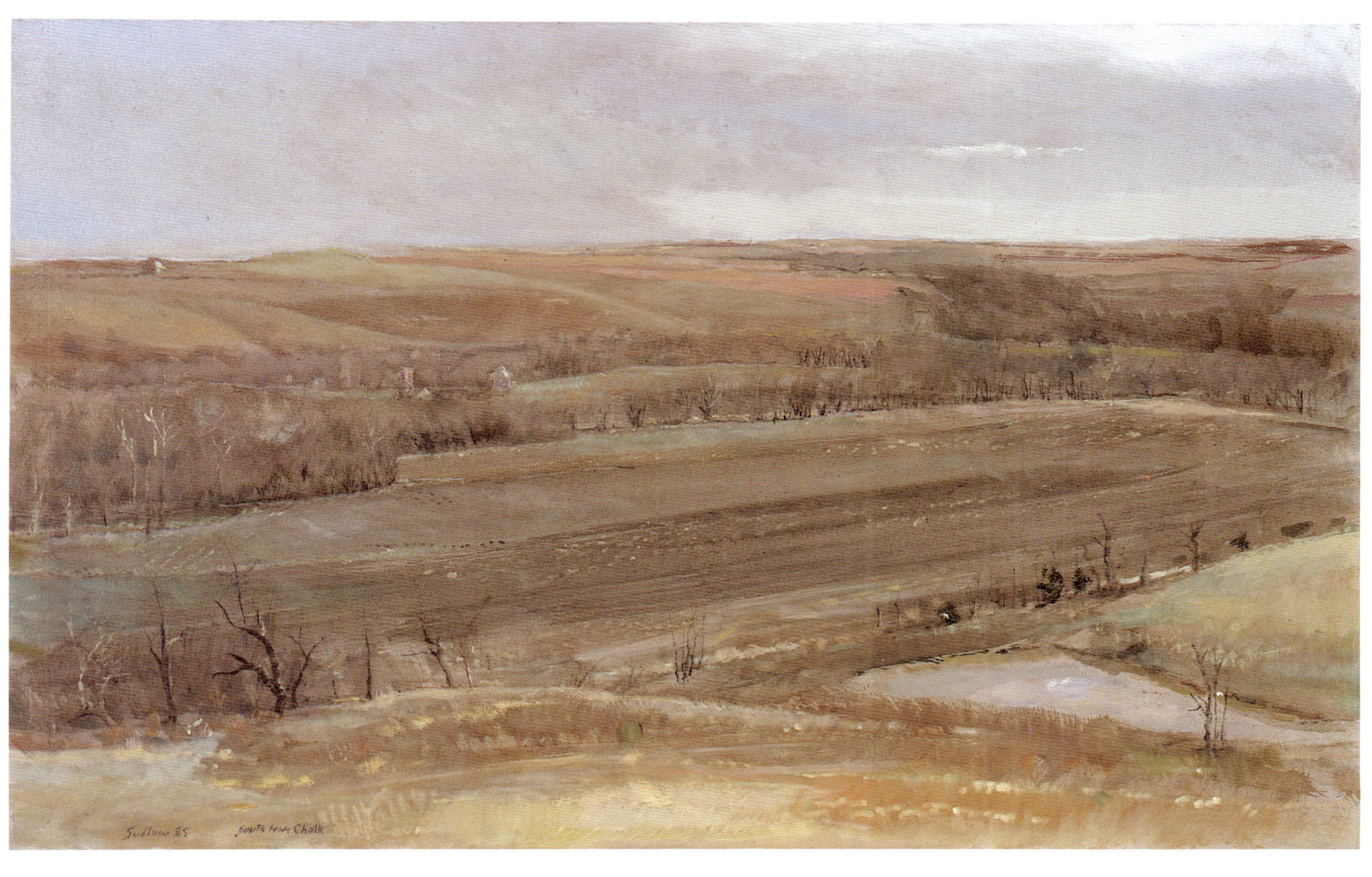

45. *South from Chalk, 1985,* 28″ × 45″
Collection of Barbara Sudlow, Lawrence, Kansas

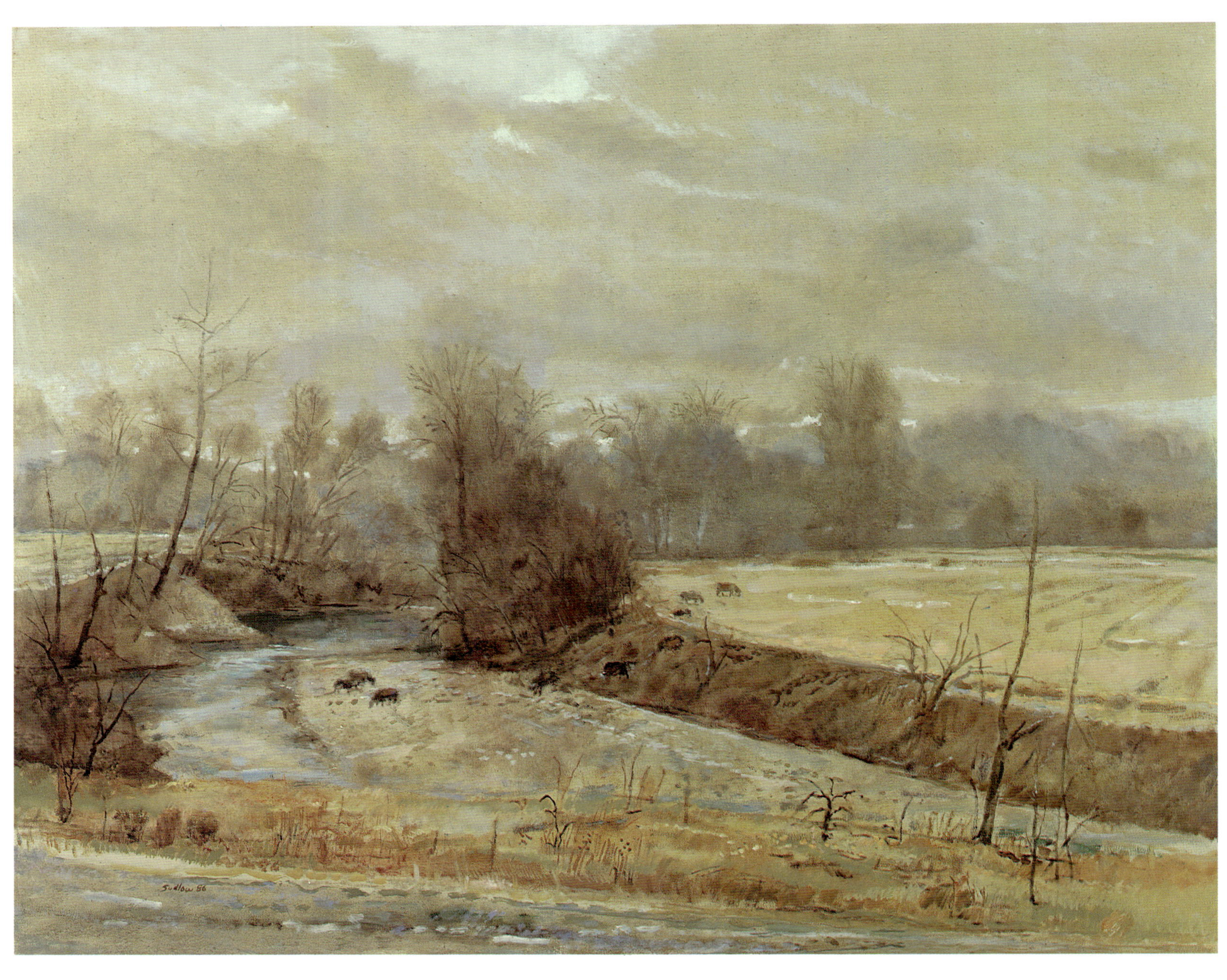

46. *Foggy Mill Creek, 1986,* 40″ × 50″
Artist's Collection

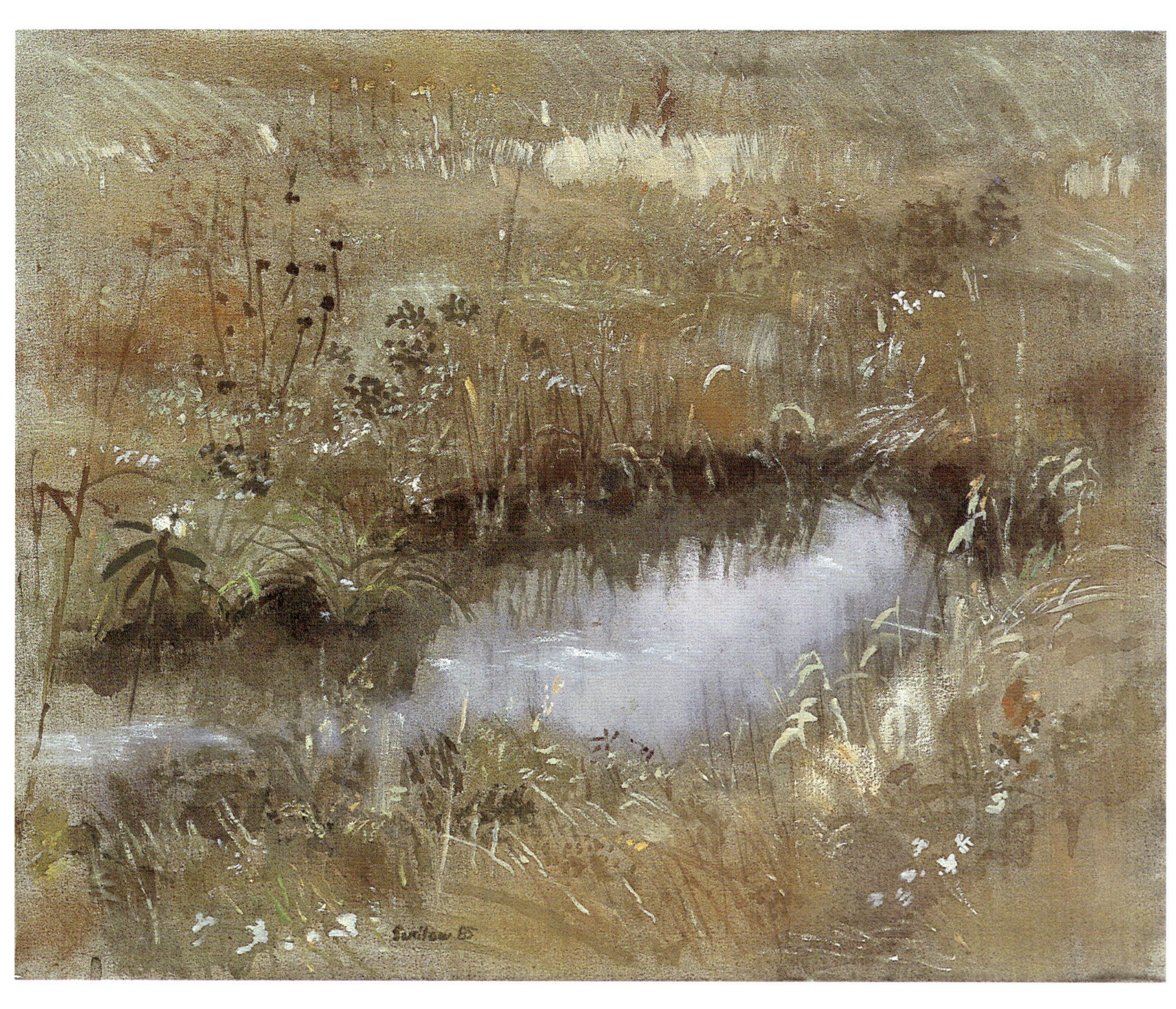

47. *Autumn Puddle, 1985,* 17″ × 20″
Artist's Collection

48. *Stull Valley, 1977,* 46″ × 42″

Collection of Mr. & Mrs. Horace Eubank, Topeka, Kansas

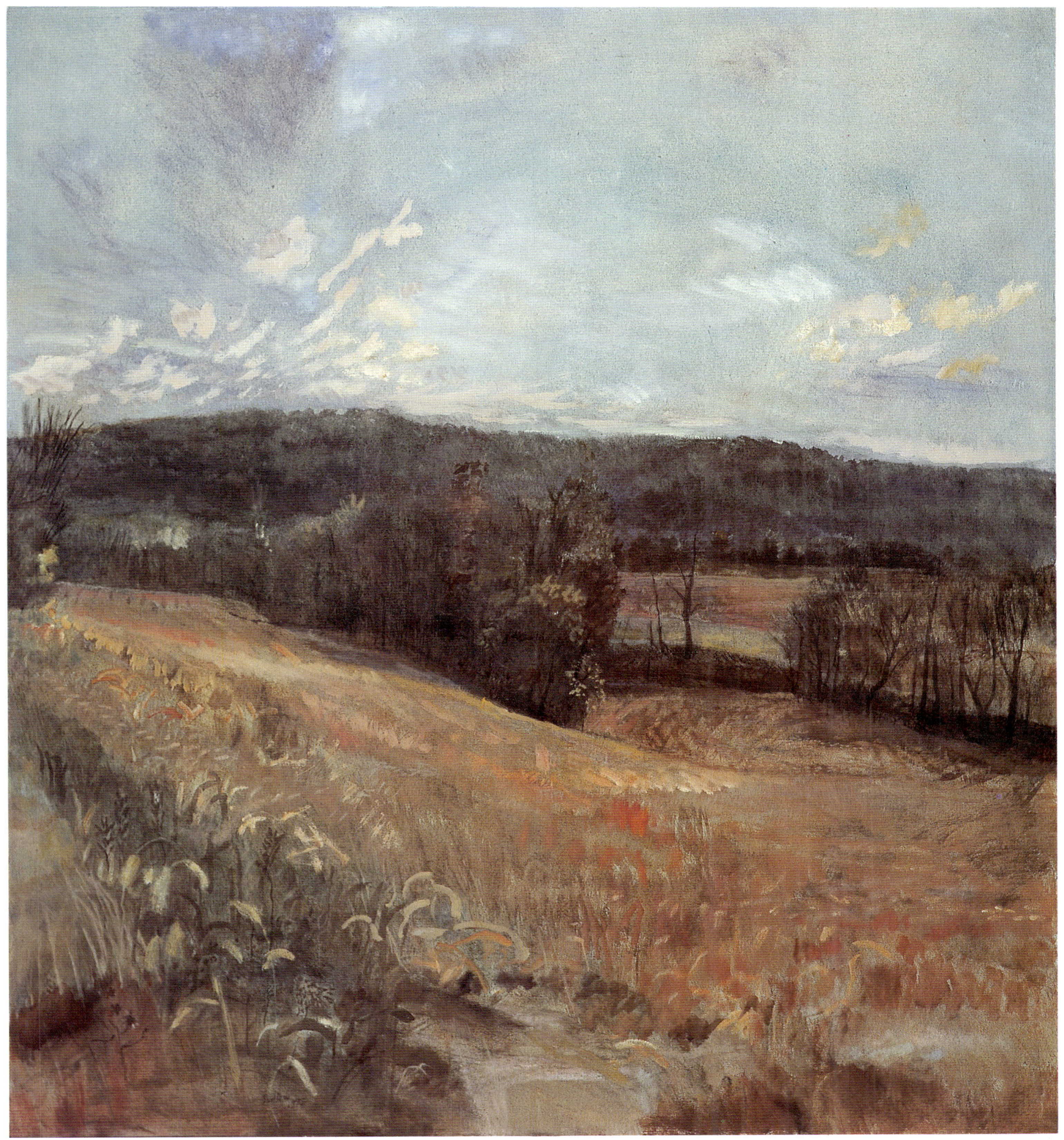

Viewed from the hill, the characteristic furniture is all in place, the panorama is immense. Hedgerows and fields, even the ugly buildings, take on order. The brown river looks grand. I am apt to speculate on the workings of those diminished farms. Distance lends a wonderful detachment. It is a setup; I grow suspicious of my place.

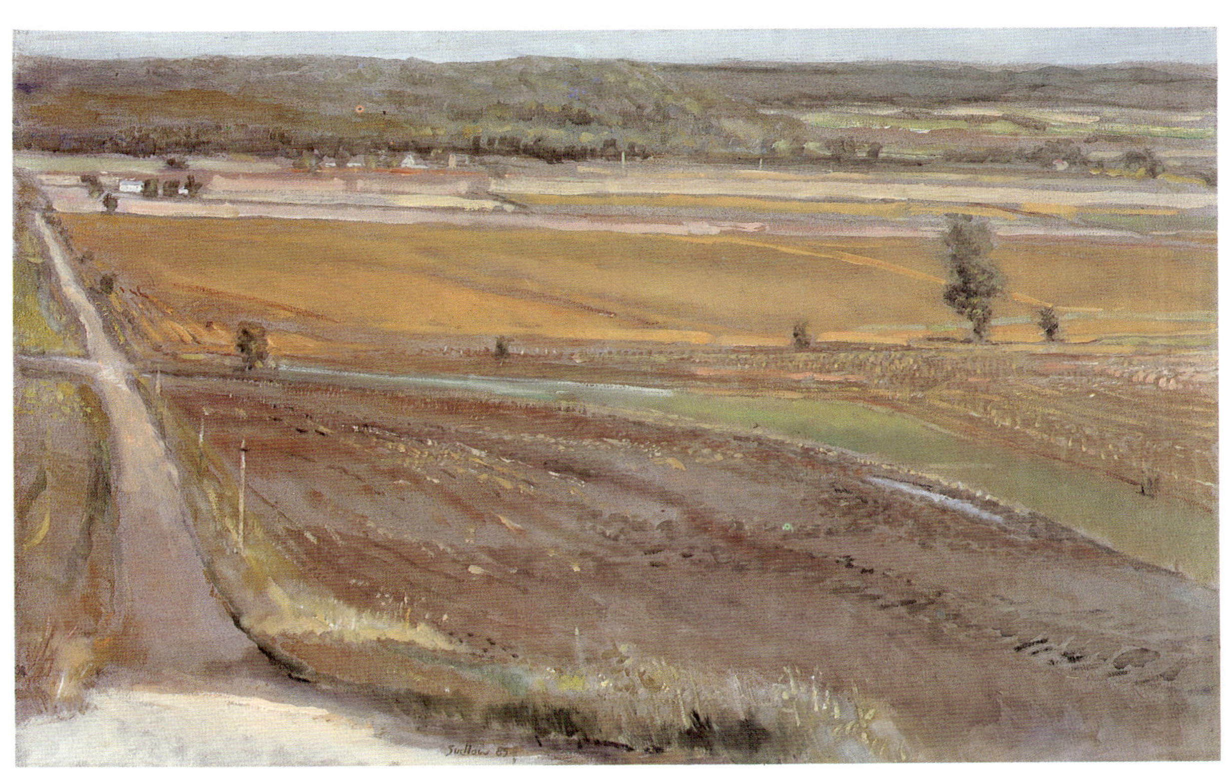

49. *Soybean Fields, 1985,* 23″ × 36″
Artist's Collection

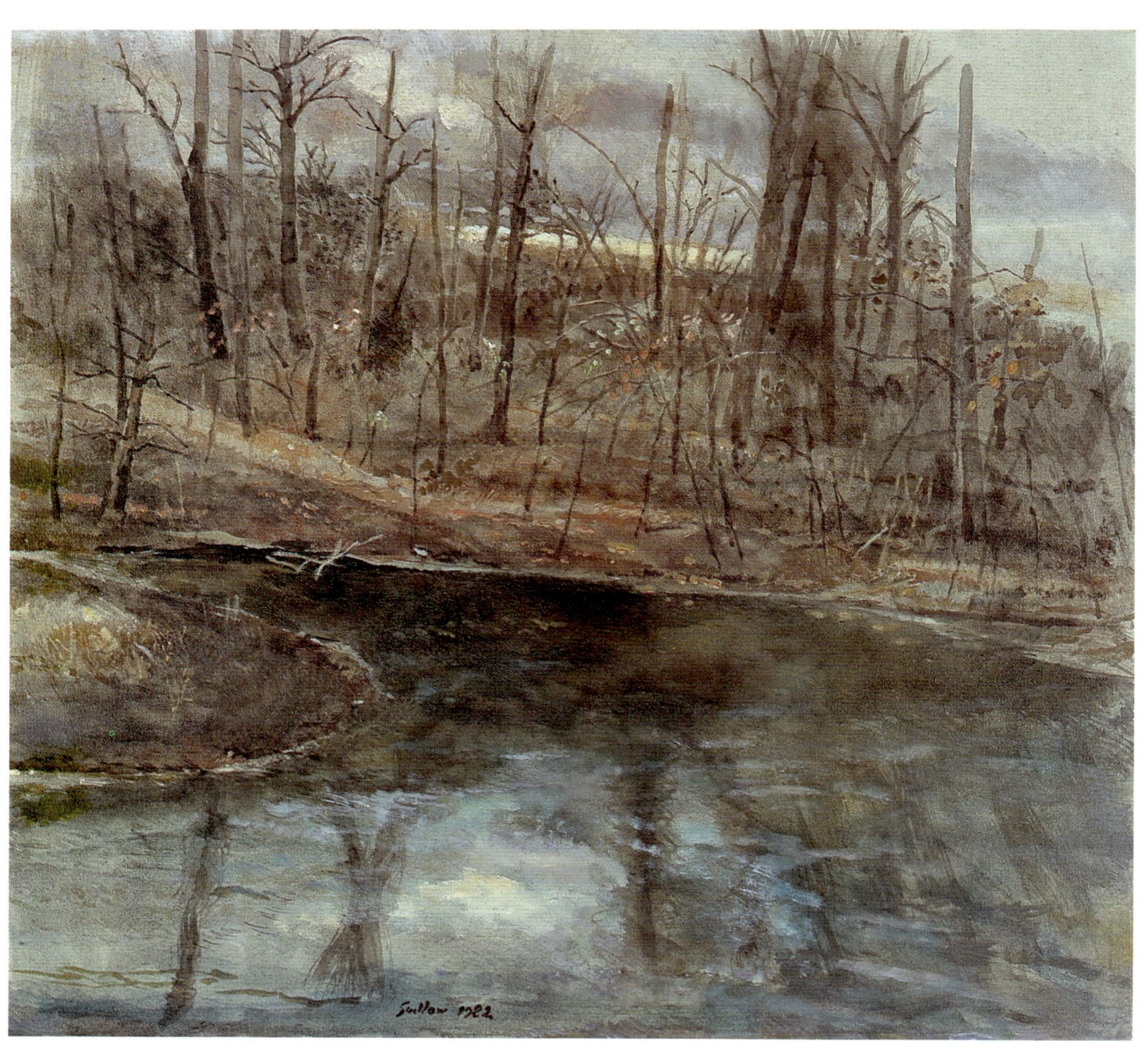

50. *Lessenden Pond, 1982,* 24″ × 26″
Artist's Collection

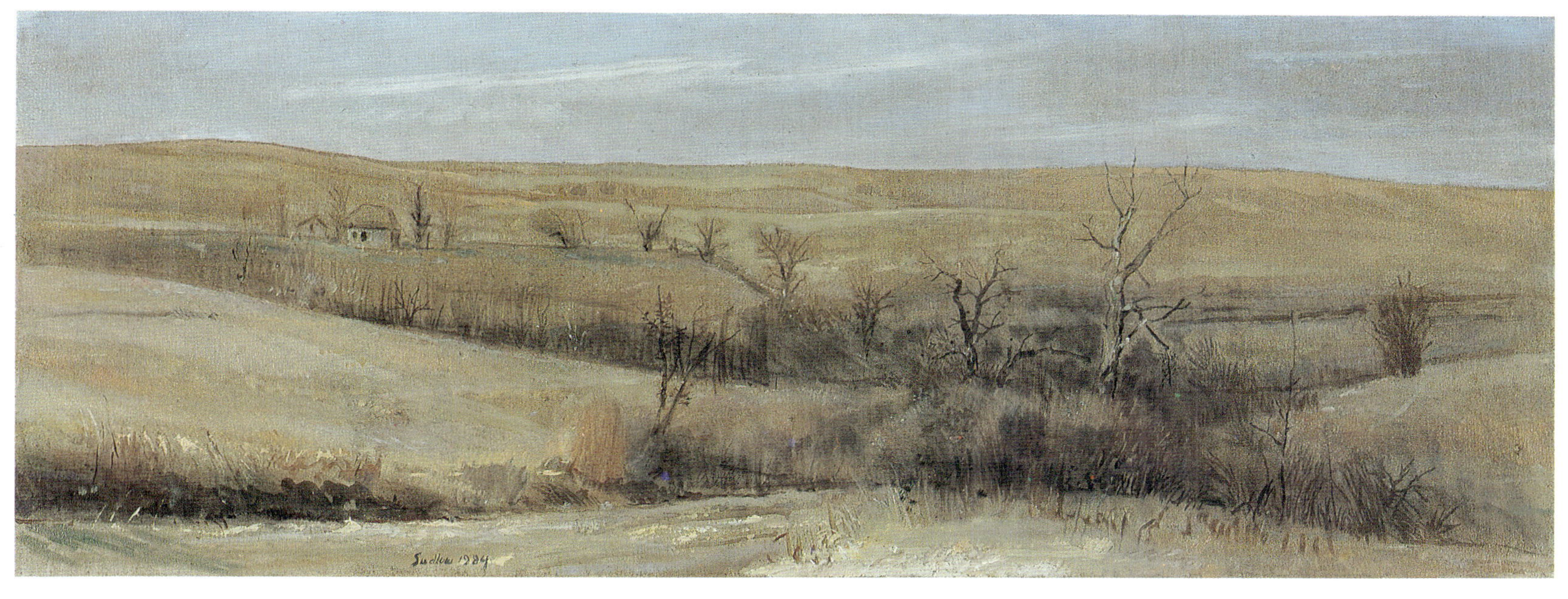

51. *Wabaunsee, North Farm, 1984,* 19″ × 42″
Collection of Mr. & Mrs. Lee Capps, Lawrence, Kansas

52. *From Hessdale West, 1985,* 44″ × 48″
American Legacy Gallery, Kansas City, Missouri

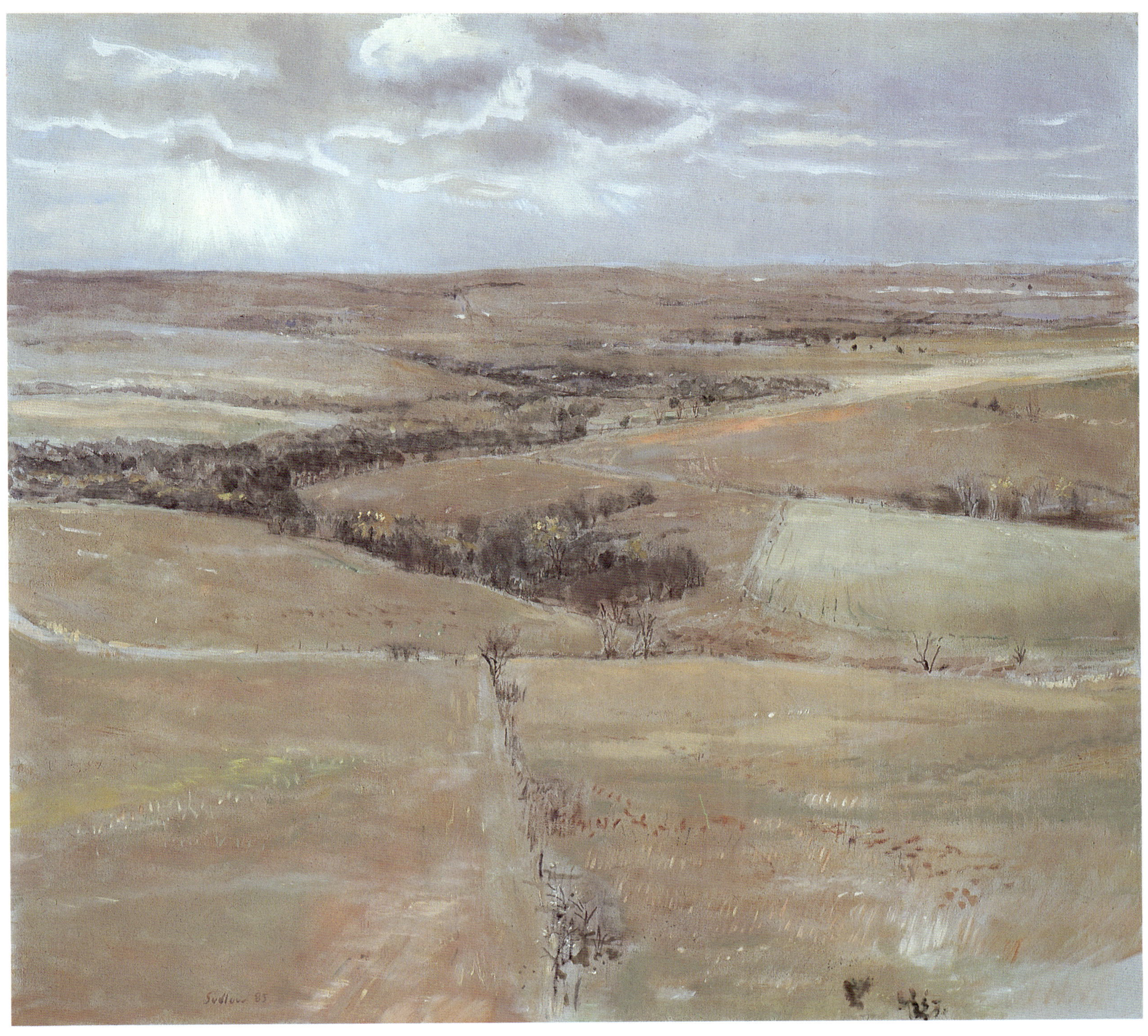

Wabaunsee County above Hessdale

A field of radiant grasses, swept to the horizon, glowing blades of bright cadmium orange cover the matted floor. High, arched clouds drift across a light-washed cerulean sky. A bunched flight of robins toss over my shoulder. This canvas vaguely echoes these events. I work frantically, knowing an hour will outstrip all my colors.

It is a great giant's backside. These sea-formed hills seem never still. From the western-shadowed slopes comes a distant concert of crow calls. The sky is a bowl brimming with clouds; light unrolls through their passage. Gradually a darkness fills the valley; the upper hills receive a final burnishing. Their furred flanks burn gold; the warm air carries cries of flying bluebirds. I sit in a theater of amber brilliance.

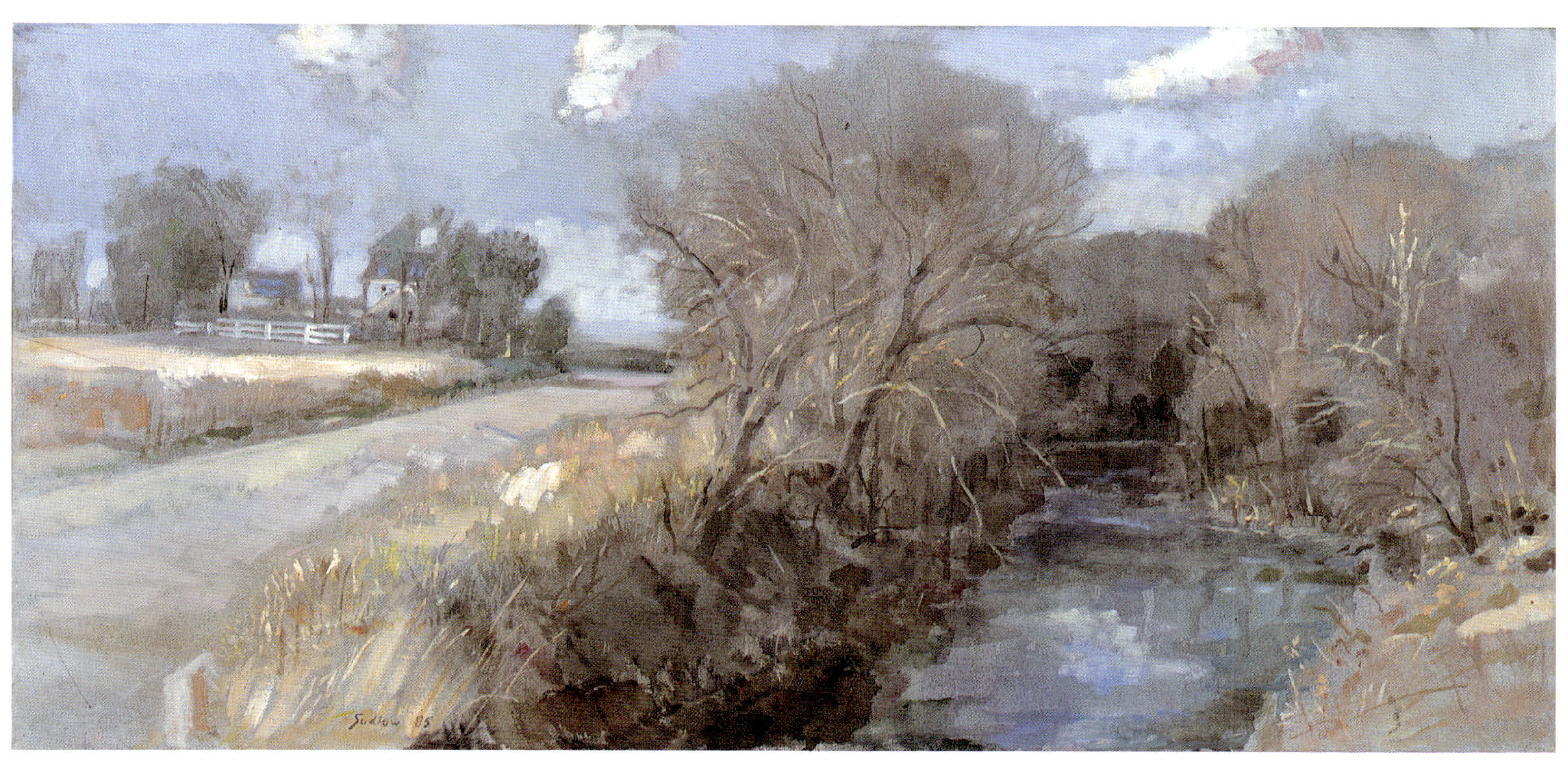

53. *Late Afternoon, Mill Creek, 1985,* 19″ × 40″
Artist's Collection

54. *Dusk, Near Stull, 1977,* 46″ × 42″

Collection of Mr. & Mrs. David Evans, Lawrence, Kansas

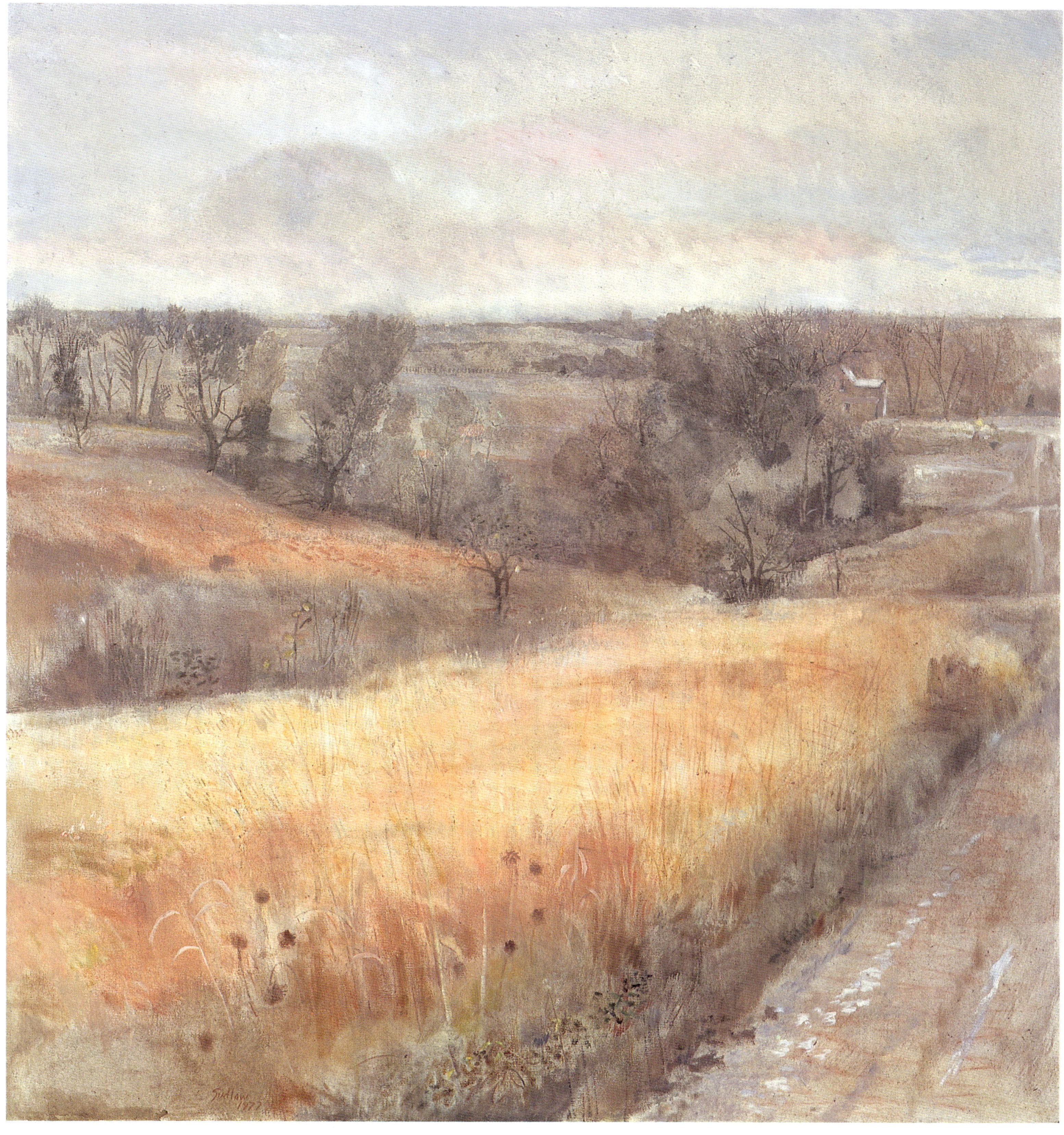